Faith Worth Defending

*How to Share your Christian
Faith in a Skeptical Culture*

Kenneth G. McLeod, PhD

Didache
Publishing House

Faith Worth Defending

Didache Publishing House
Atlanta, Georgia
Printed in the U.S.A.

ESV - Scripture quotations are from The Holy Bible, English Standard Version® (ESV®), copyright © 2001 by Crossway, a publishing ministry of Good News Publishers. Used by permission. All rights reserved.

ISBN-13: 978-1505966169
ISBN-10: 1505966167

To My Wife, Susan

Contents

Faith Worth Defending

INTRODUCTION

"It's no longer enough to teach our children Bible stories; they need doctrine and apologetics."

— William Lane Craig, PhD

Not long ago I was teaching an apologetics class to a small group that was meeting in a church member's home. This was a typical small group of adults; all Christians, most married, but with one exception: this group included two women married to unbelieving skeptical husbands who would have nothing to do with the church.

One night after finishing the lecture, I was gathering my materials and preparing to leave. One of the women married to a skeptic approached me and said,

"Can I ask you a question?"

"Of course" I said, "What's on your mind?"

With a broken look on her face, she explained how she had tried to talk to her husband about God and get him into church, but with no success. It was clear that she loved her husband very much and wanted to share her Christian life with him, but she could not get him to move even one centimeter in the direction of the church because of his skepticism. She felt defeated.

I discovered that she tried to get him to read the Bible, hoping that would be the catalyst for his conversion. I explained that with skeptics, like her husband, this usually gets you nowhere. I suggested several ways to start a conversation that might get him talking and engaged on the subject of God's existence, which he doubted. She was encouraged by what I told her and seemed hopeful. After promising to put her new knowledge into practice, she got in her car and left.

To this day, I have no idea if this lady has made any progress with her husband. Maybe that's not what you expected of this story. Sure, I could tell a similar story where the person came back to me later with a positive report, even a salvation story. But the point I want to make here is that upon learning a few things about defending the faith, her hope was renewed. She was bolder and more willing to go back in and try again. That gives me great encouragement. It must, because skeptics can be hard to convince; many have even hardened their hearts to the point of no return. As God said, *"My Spirit shall not always strive with man"*

(Genesis 6:3). Nevertheless, we are to spread the Gospel of Jesus Christ and, in doing so, defend the faith.

This type of spiritual concern for a family member is very common. Many times it's a close friend or co-worker, but the story is the same - A Christian having difficulty dealing with skepticism and doubt from a friend or family member. The problem is, they lack the basic training in Christian apologetics to deal with these issues. So what is apologetics?

Apologetics means defending the faith by offering rational arguments for the existence of God, the rationale for Christianity, and the validity of the Bible. In this context, 'argument' does not mean a brawl, but a thoughtful explanation of the evidence that demonstrates how we know that our faith in God is true. The word apologetics comes from the Greek word apologia, which means "to give a defense." It does not mean that Christians are apologizing for anything. It's better illustrated by thinking about a lawyer making a defense for a client in court. If the lawyer wants to be successful, evidence must be presented that comes from reliable eyewitness testimony, authentic documents, and scientific facts. Simply claiming the client is innocent will not convince a jury any more than simply claiming that God exists will convince a skeptic. It eventually comes down to the evidence.

Having said that, always remember that we use apologetics to share the evidence of Christianity with skeptics. We use it to convince those who are not convinced. On the other hand, if someone wants to talk to you about God, Jesus or the Bible with an open mind, or if they are sincerely seeking the truth, then your testimony as a Christian is probably all you need. The person who is seeking answers about God needs to hear your personal story and see how God has changed your life. After all, the presence of the Holy Spirit living within you is the most powerful evidence for your faith.

Of course, not everyone is sincerely seeking answers with an open heart. Not everyone understands what it means to experience the Holy Spirit. Some are skeptical, but willing to talk; some will refuse to discuss matters of God; and some are hostile towards Christianity and only seek to defeat you in an argument. Either way, we have a duty to spread the Gospel throughout the world. In doing so, this will require defending the faith to skeptics and making a case for the hope we have in Jesus.

> *"And always be ready to give a defense to everyone who asks you a reason for the hope that is in you."*
> -1 Peter 3:15

With a basic knowledge of apologetics, you can make a case for the existence of God, the truth of Christianity, and the authenticity of the Bible. The material in this book can give you the confidence to explain why you believe what you believe while sharing the Gospel of Jesus Christ. It can help you become a bolder witness for Christ because you will have the evidence to back up your claim that

Christianity is the only path to God. After all, without evidence to offer the skeptic, you will sound just like every other religion out there competing for believers with nothing more than "it's true because we say it's true."

This book can also help you answer your own tough questions without depending on shallow answers or running from your own skepticism. I have found that most thinking people are skeptical by nature; so if you feel that your own questions about God, Jesus and the Bible were never fully answered in Sunday school, church, or by your Christian friends, then keep reading. This book is intended to treat you like a critical thinker who can handle the truth. You should consider this book a safe place where you can work through your own doubts and questions. Let's face it, you can't make a case for Christianity until you can answer your own questions; and you need to be able to make a case because the Word of God instructs us to do so.

".... knowing that I am put here for the defense of the gospel."

- Philippians 1:16

The Culture

I was recently in a radio station preparing for an apologetics program. As I was preparing to go on the air, a technician who worked there asked me, "what is apologetics?" I explained that apologetics involves offering rational evidence for the existence of God, the authenticity of Christianity and the reliability of the Bible. His response was, "Oh, you mean that stuff we should believe by faith?"

Although I tried not to show it, I'm always concerned about Christians who make comments like that. To ignore the evidence for our faith while talking to others about Jesus makes Christians sound just like every other religion, and cult, in the world. Furthermore, to ignore the evidence for our faith is to depart from the methods used by Paul (1 Corinthians 15:4-8), Luke (Acts 1:3), Peter (1 Peter 3:15) and Jesus (John 10:25).

The fact is, people are more skeptical today than ever before. To tell a skeptic to believe in God because we say so will not work. Just because the Christian has the self-authenticating witness of the Holy Spirit living in them does not mean that an unbeliever will be impressed. For many people, evidence matters. We cannot simply tell people to believe because we say it's true - that's what the Mormons do (and Jehovah's Witness and many others).

I'm not making the case that evidence will save anyone, it will not. The Holy Spirit must be at work in the skeptic's life to draw him to Christ. However, many people have become Christians after pondering the evidence. The support for the claims of Jesus, once fully reviewed, have sent many running to the cross. This makes sense because many ex-skeptics report they had never really considered the evidence. After doing so, they were compelled to trust in Jesus.

8

It's easy to argue that the culture demands evidence; but at the same time, one may argue that the culture runs from it as well. This type of thing happens in a culture of sexual promiscuity where so many are hooked on money, hero worship and self-gratification. In this culture, I would argue that many people are just as afraid of the evidence for Christianity as they are skeptical of it.

For example, I was recently talking to a gentleman I met while out of town. We had a pleasant conversation and he seemed to be an intelligent person. I asked him about God and he replied, "I don't believe in God, I believe in evolution."

Based on that statement, I knew he had never given this very much thought. So I asked: "Why do you choose evolution over God?" He looked uncomfortable and started explaining that he had adopted a personal policy not to discuss such matters. I was surprised because he seemed so willing to discuss frivolous matters, but not something important. Although I cannot read minds, it seemed clear that he was afraid of discussing the evidence for God's existence.

In a way, it makes sense that some atheists and skeptics would feel this way. After all, if God exists then it's a scary thought. It means we are accountable to Him and will one day be judged. It also means, to many people, that they will have to give up their lifestyle and bend a knee. Many will not even entertain that thought.

So it seems that we, Christians, are working against a huge cultural tidal wave that rushes in the opposite direction of the Church. Therefore, to spread the Gospel of Jesus Christ without knowing how to share the evidences of our faith could lead to drowning.

Faith and Reason

People reject the existence of God and the teachings of Christ for various reasons. For some it's rational, and their arguments always point to insufficient evidence. Others have an emotional response that leads them to reject God based on their dislike of God, or dislike of Christians. This may stem from the acts of Christians throughout history, or from the Christian living next door.

The new atheists, who are better classified as anti-theists, claim there is no evidence for the existence of God, and as a result, argue that all faith is blind faith. They ignore the mounds of evidence for God's existence while accepting the paltry evidence that life evolved from non-life. They also ignore the widely understood (and practiced) definition of faith, which means 'trust.'

Christian faith is not blind faith, it is faith based on reason. However, the new atheists have set their focus on painting all faith as mere superstition. Unfortunately, this is an effective strategy because so many Christians are only able to defend their faith by invoking their faith. Meaning, they are good at talking about what they believe, but not why they believe it outside of the framework of faith.

Of course, faith (not blind faith) is an absolute

necessity of the Christian life. Christian faith is very personal and self-authenticating. Nevertheless, Christians may need to justify what that faith is based upon if they are actively spreading the Gospel. It's not very convincing to a skeptic when we say, "*I know Christianity is true because I feel it.*" Remember, the skeptic does not "*feel it*" yet.

This is why we have to be mindful about how we feel about our own faith and how it is viewed by the new atheists. One of the most important arguments against Christianity today is that faith is blind, unfounded, and a delusion. We know that characterization of faith is a straw man argument, but we still have to be prepared to deal with it.

One of the most important early church leaders and thinkers was St. Augustin of Hippo (354AD-430AD) who said, "*Faith first, then reason.*" This means that we need faith as Christians to turn from sin and accept Christ as savior. But once that is done, we can apply reason to what we believe and realize that Christianity explains reality better than any other worldview.

Hundreds of years earlier, in the second century, Justin Martyr (100AD-165AD) explained the process between faith and reason for the Christian:

> *A man seeks the truth by the unaided effort of reason and is disappointed.*
>
> *The truth is offered to him by faith, and he accepts.*
>
> *And, having accepted, he finds that it satisfies his reason.*

This is important to understand because the new atheists will challenge your ability to reason if you claim to be a Christian. In other words, you are just an irrational person who believes in fairytales. Of course, this is an absurd challenge; but if you don't know why this is an absurd challenge, you can be caught off guard. Remember, if you cannot stand your ground, it will be pulled out from under you.

Some of the greatest scientists and philosophers that ever lived were Christians. Moreover, many of the world's great scientists who live today are Christians. For an atheist to say that all of these people are irrational is a bold statement that cannot possibly be supported by the facts. It's an attack on the person, not the facts - a common technique used by atheists. This is interesting because atheists will tell you they are the keepers of reason, but as soon as the debate over God begins, many abandon reason and resort to personal attacks. This is not arguing from a position of reason and logic, it's a street corner brawl. Of course, not all atheists argue this way, but the new atheists are more aggressive in their opinions and totally intolerant of Christianity.

What is Truth?

Remember, you not only need to have faith to be a Christian, you need to be able to defend that faith with reasonable arguments. Sure, you believe Christianity is true, but how do you respond to your atheist neighbor's claim that there is no absolute truth?

Unfortunately, too many people today take a relative approach to truth. After all, if no one has the truth, then you can make up your own truth and live as you want. That philosophy appeals to many young people, some of whom even claim that truth is what feels good. However, before you get too frustrated with this absurd version of the truth, you should respond to the statement - "There is no absolute truth" with, "Is that statement absolutely true?"

When you are informed by the modern thinker that, in the area of God and faith, we cannot know anything for certain, you should ask, "Are you certain about that?" You see, the truth is like a brick wall, you can ignore it, or walk around it, but you can't run right through it without getting a bloody nose. Even so, it is very trendy in some circles today to deny the existence of absolute truth. This opposition can be stated as:

There is no such thing as truth.
All truth is subjective.
No one has the truth.
That can be true for you but not for me.
All truth is relative and depends on your personal perspective.

We can easily refute the idea of subjective truth and demonstrate the absurdity of this philosophy. For example, in reference to the aforementioned five objections to truth, when someone declares, "There is no such thing as objective truth," one may respond with, "Then how can your statement be true? If there is no truth, then your statement, 'there is no truth', must also not be true." Therefore, the statement "There is no truth" is a self-defeating proposition that refutes itself.

By the same logic, the statement "All truth is subjective" cannot be accepted because that would make the statement that "All truth is subjective" a subjective statement that is invalid and should be ignored. Likewise, when presented with the argument, "No one has the truth," we should inquire, "Then how do you know your statement that 'no one has the truth' is true since you obviously do not possess the truth either based on your own argument."

The fourth objection, "Something can be true for you but not for me," can be answered with the question, "Is your statement, 'something can be true for you but not for me', only true for you and not me, or anyone else?" And the last point, "All truth is relative and depends on your personal perspective," should be answered, "Is that statement relative and only based on your personal perspective?"

It becomes clear that when philosophers attempt to define truth as non-objective they are forced to use an objective truth argument to maintain their position. This line of thinking is the pinnacle of arrogance because it assumes that one can make statements about the absence of objective truth, while somehow standing outside reality where they can see a truth that no one else can see. This is an example of making an argument against objective truth using objective truth. The end result is a flawed argument that becomes circular and quickly defeats itself.

When Reason Fails

In his 1942 satirical Christian apologetic novel, *The Screwtape Letters*, C.S. Lewis tells the story of a demon named Screwtape who is counseling an inexperienced younger demon, named wormwood, on the finer points of keeping mankind from God.

> *"Jargon, not argument, is your best ally in keeping him from the Church. Don't waste time trying to make him think that materialism is true! Make him think it is strong, or stark, or courageous-that it is the philosophy of the future. That's the sort of thing he cares about..."*

Screwtape goes on to explain that logical argument is ineffective against the believer because it risks waking up the person's reason, and that is to be avoided. At one point in the book he says:

> *"The best of all is to let him read no science but to give him a grand general idea that he knows it all and that everything he happens to have picked up in casual talk and reading is the result of modern investigation"*

This is very prophetic for a book written in 1942 before the age of the internet, where young and old alike are 'picking up' misleading arguments from poorly educated atheists on the merits of God's existence. Very few of these arguments make a rational case against the existence of God, but instead attempt to make atheism appear to be more intelligent, more rational, and totally hip. The leaders of the new atheists go even further by abandoning argumentation completely and resorting to insults. For example, at the annual reason rally in Washington, DC, Richard Dawkins fired up the crowd by declaring that atheists should show contempt for believers, not respect. He said:

> "Mock them! Ridicule them! In public. Don't fall for the convention that we're all too polite to talk about religion. Religion is not off the table. Religion is not off the list. Religion makes specific claims about the universe which need to be substantiated, and need to be challenged, and if necessary, need to be ridiculed with contempt."

Atheists like Dawkins have no desire to answer the specific truth claims made by Christians, so they resort to mockery and ridicule while claiming no evidence exists. This fits the model described by Lewis in the 40s: don't engage the Christian intellectually, just promote atheism as the future and religion as irrational.

Dawkins and other atheists may not like the evidence that is presented for God's existence, and they may not accept it, but a response like the one described here is not a rational defense, it's a school-yard insult that should be beneath someone claiming to be a scientist.

Faith Worth Defending

As you can see, and probably already know, you have a battle ahead of you if you want to convince people in our skeptical culture that Jesus is Lord. I think many Christians today feel like they are living in two different worlds as a citizen of modern America, and as a Christian.

As a Christian surrounded by non-believers in a culture that is more and more hostile to your beliefs, you will need to stand firm in your faith while defending it. This may not be a problem, depending on what you already know about apologetics. However, it could be a real challenge. Either way, the purpose of this book is to help you maintain perspective in the face of intellectual pressure.

> *"Let us hold fast the confession of our hope without wavering, for he who promised is faithful."*
> -Hebrews 10:23

Christianity is under fire more than ever. America is in moral decay and dragging most of the population down a dark path. God points out our sin, shines a light on it, and people don't like that very much. In some circles, that can make you extremely unpopular. But as the Bible says, hold fast without wavering and you will be strengthened even more.

In your day to day life, you can keep quiet or share your faith. There are times when keeping quiet will be necessary. Remember, 1 Peter 3:15 instructs us to

"...*always be ready to give an answer to everyone who asks*..." Some people don't ask. Some people don't want to know, and they will get angry if you press them on the subject. I know, I've done it. So we need to walk wise when sharing and engaging skeptics with the gospel so that we do not fall into pointless squabbles with those who only want to beat us in an argument, not listen to what we have to say about God.

On the other hand, if you are struggling with your faith or do not believe in God, then please consider what is offered in the following chapters. If you are skeptical, then take some time off to be skeptical of your own skepticism. After all, looking at both sides with an open mind is what a reasonable person does, right?

Please keep in mind that if you want to reject God, you will find a way - that is certain. Human beings have an amazing ability to see truth in anything they want. This type of biased thinking should be obvious, but it's not always that easy. However, when you see truth where you don't expect it, then slow down and take notice - it may be something other than bias. Many skeptics who come to Christ describe it that way. They did not want the truth to be there, but it was.

Whatever we believe, evidence should play a role in that belief. Otherwise, we are merely engaged in superstition. That is something we should never be. Faith in God is not superstition, and faith in God never stopped anyone from asking questions, seeking knowledge, or finding answers.

CHAPTER ONE

Does God Exist?

"The atheist can't find God for the same reason that a thief can't find a policeman."

-Author Unknown

At some point we all hear this question: *"Can you prove that God exists?"* Or maybe you've heard someone say: *"I don't believe in God because there is not enough evidence."* Of course, the existence of God cannot be proven in the same manner that we can prove 2+2=4, but the same applies to many other things people believe, such as the origin of the universe and the origin of biological life.

Even so, there are many lines of evidence for the existence of God; some have been around for thousands of years. These various arguments are strong on their own, but together they form a powerful cumulative case for God's existence. Nevertheless, the new atheists are still finding ways to undermine belief in God for their growing audience of book readers and convention attendees.

Although atheists make up a small population of the world, their numbers are growing – especially in Europe and the United States. While atheism has not grown at the rates predicted one hundred years ago, it is vocal, out front, in style, and aggressive. Therefore, Christians cannot sit back and allow atheists to frame the debate on God. We must present sound arguments that make a case for God in a culture where so much confusion has been intentionally introduced by the shrill voice of atheism.

What is Atheism?

Atheism can be defined more than one way. Typically, Christians define it as someone who denies God exists. This is usually true, but the new atheists do not seem to like that definition and claim it only describes a small minority of atheists. They prefer to define atheism as, "The lack of belief in gods." With this definition, atheists feel they don't have to prove anything because they are not asserting anything. They are simply saying they don't believe in any gods, and nothing else. Of course, there are major problems with this definition. I will give you two.

First, the lack-of-belief-in-gods definition means

that the atheist is not asserting anything along with their atheism. In other words, they are not attaching any other beliefs to the claim that they don't believe in God. If that is true, then atheism is not pro-science, or pro-reason, or pro-logic, or pro-anything. If an atheist happens to be pro-science, or pro-reason, then it has nothing to do with their atheism. Based on their definition, these things are non-atheist views. As a result, atheists should stop claiming that atheism is the only rational worldview.

Worse, the atheist's self-definition makes no moral claim whatsoever. If an atheist happens to be a good person, or believes in treating others with respect or kindness, it has nothing to do with their atheism. Moral laws and moral duties are non-atheist views.

Furthermore, atheists claim that belief in God is a comfortable position and people use it as a crutch, especially when it comes to the fear of dying. The former governor of Minnesota, Jesse Ventura, said, "Organized religion is a sham and a crutch for weak-minded people who need strength in numbers." Other celebrities have made similar comments, like Ted Turner and Bill Maher. These atheists want to pretend they have no need for such weak-minded institutions. But do they?

C.S. Lewis said that he did not choose Christianity to make him happy or feel good, a bottle of booze would do that. He recommended a different path for those who want a religion that makes them feel good and comfortable. Although the God of Christianity is a loving God, He is also demanding, jealous, and will judge everyone for their sins. Therefore, choosing Christianity is not choosing comfort, but choosing to follow the commandments of God.

On the other hand, atheism has no commandments, no rules, no requirements - no nothing! Therefore, if you want a really big comfortable crutch, try atheism.

Lines of Evidence

Making a cumulative case for God's existence takes time. You cannot do it between floors on an elevator. As a result, we have to decide what to talk to atheists about, and what evidence to present, in order to make the most of our time. That information is found in the strategies chapter of this book and it can teach you how to approach skeptics. Nevertheless, once you find yourself in conversation with an atheist, it is important to know the major arguments.

I have found as many as twenty different arguments for the existence of God. Some have overlapping concepts, some are quite unique, and others are very esoteric and complex. For example, as far back as Aristotle in ancient Greece, philosophers have discussed the need for a first cause of everything (cosmological argument). Some of the first Christians argued for the existence of God based on a set of reasons why God must exist (ontological argument). The earliest philosophically rigorous version of the design argument (teleological argument) came from St. Thomas Aquinas (1225-1274). In modern times, the design argument has developed into the intelligent design argument based, primarily, on the information found in DNA.

Other arguments for the existence of God focus on morality, human consciousness, mathematical truths, metaphysical concepts, and human experience. The point is, there are a lot of well-defined reasons to believe that God exists. Should you use them all? Probably not. The fact is, you will most likely never get a chance to use all of these arguments with any atheist you encounter. In my experience, there are a few strong arguments that are good to know and easy to use, so I will cover them here. These arguments fall into three main categories: Cosmological, design, and moral.

The Cosmological Argument

If we argue that life did not arise through natural, unguided, unintelligent means by chance, the only other alternative is design. The question is: who is the designer? We can start by considering that design did not begin with life, but with the formation of the universe. Therefore, the universe also needed a designer. This is evident in that the universe not only appears designed, but functions as if designed. Not only that, the universe came into existence at some point and therefore must have a cause. Arguing that the universe has a cause is called the Cosmological Argument, and this argument makes a strong case for the existence of God.

The Cosmological Argument for the existence of

God offers powerful evidence for a creator and is easy to understand in its basic form. It goes like this:

Premise 1 - Whatever begins to exist has a cause.
Premise 2 - The universe began to exist.
Conclusion - Therefore, the universe had a cause.

Causation is a fundamental principal of science. In fact, cause and effect is what science is all about. When we understand the cause of some phenomenon, we can understand the phenomenon better. For example, there was a time when people believed that lightning was the wrath of the gods. After gaining a basic understanding of electricity and meteorology, human beings now know that lighting is merely an electrical reaction to charged particles in the sky. In other words, we know what causes lighting.

For hundreds of years, scientists believed that the universe did not have a cause, but that it always existed. This was called steady state cosmology. About sixty years ago, that was replaced with big bang cosmology. The beginning point of the universe is now seen as the big bang by modern science, but with no meaningful explanation of what caused the big bang to bang. Interestingly, Jews and Christians have been claiming for thousands of years that the universe had a beginning; now, modern science has come to that same conclusion via the big bang theory. And if we accept the big bang theory, then we accept that the universe exploded into existence in a fraction of a second. That sounds a lot like Genesis 1.

In the beginning, God created the heavens and the Earth.

- Genesis 1:1 (ESV)

But, why does this have to involve God? Because it seems clear from observation that nothing pops into existence for no reason and without cause. Causality is an absolute law of science and absolutely necessary for scientific discovery. If something begins to exists, it resulted from a cause.

We know that the universe had a beginning; therefore, something must have caused it to begin. The explanation for the cause behind the cause is explained by showing that only a transcendent being that resides outside of time and space and not affected by the laws of nature could have caused the universe and everything in it to exist. After all, how could something that is part of the universe cause the universe? That would be the same as the universe having its own cause, and nothing can cause itself to exist. Could you cause yourself to exist? Of course not. You are the product of your parents, and they were caused by their parents and on and on until we get all the way back to the first uncaused cause.

There is agreement in the scientific community that before the big bang, nothing existed in the universe - not matter, space or even time. Therefore, whatever caused the big bang to bang must stand outside of time and space. But what if the cause of the big bang had a cause, then we have no need for God, right? Not so fast. If the big bang had a natural cause that does not involve the direct work of God, then science demands that whatever the cause may be must also, itself, have a cause. You see the problem? We are caught in an infinite regress of causes that never ends. Now we have a major problem; specifically, that time cannot regress backwards into infinity. If time stretches back for an infinite number of days, then we would never have reached this point in time, because to do so would require crossing an infinite number of days, which is impossible.

Of course, the major problem is that we need an uncaused first cause. We need something that is eternal, immaterial, atemporal, non-spatial, and uncaused. In other words, we need something that cannot not exist. Based on the premise of the argument, it's logical to conclude that only God can fit the description. Specifically, the God of Christianity since His attributes have been described this way from the beginning. So when atheists argue that belief in God is a blind leap of faith, be assured that it is not. Just because someone does not like the conclusion of an argument based on a sound premise, does not make the argument invalid.

There is no doubt that we have good evidence from physical science and philosophy to determine that the universe had a beginning and the beginning was caused. One might still contend that the conclusion of the cosmological argument, that the cause was intelligent, is flawed. After all, maybe some unintelligent natural force created the universe and existed in the moment before the big bang. However, the problem with this line of thinking is that anything that exists outside of time and space cannot be called natural since all the natural forces and laws that govern the universe exist within the universe. Therefore, attempting to apply these natural forces to the creation of the universe, a time before natural forces existed, is an irrational argument.

In addition, the ultimate cause of the universe had to be intelligent for a couple of reasons. First, the cause had to decide to bring the universe into existence. This seems clear. If the cause of the universe was some unintelligent force unknown to science that caused the creation of the universe, or big bang, then it would either be the same age as the universe, or caused itself to exist, and we are right back to the problem of cause and effect and infinite regress. The reason is simple, if the cause of the universe was a force powerful enough to initiate the big bang, then it would have caused the big bang as soon as it came in contact with the initial matter and energy that exploded in that first nanosecond. Meaning, as soon as it appeared, the universe would appear via the big bang. This unintelligent force would not wait and decide to initiate the big bang; the bang would just happen as soon as this force was present. This can be compared to the way gravity works. When gravity is present, your feet stick to the ground. This does not happen an hour later when gravity decides to start working.

The fact is, we must have a first uncaused cause to avoid infinite regress, and this uncaused cause must have decided to start the creation event, whatever that first event happened to be - the big bang, or the cause of the big bang.

The Design Argument: Simply Analogy

Successive arguments grew out of Aquinas' work and have evolved to become more sophisticated through means of philosophical arguments and new scientific discoveries. By the 17th century the argument from simple analogy was being used by Christian apologists to oppose the onslaught of prominent atheist philosophers. The British botanist John Ray (1627-1705) in his book *The Wisdom of God Manifested in the Works of the Creation* (1601) helped promote the analogy argument. This form of the argument maintains that the world, upon close analysis, seems to demonstrate the same type of precision and design that man-made objects illustrate.

I come now to take a view of the works of creation and to observe something of the wisdom of God discernible in the formation of them in their order and harmony (Ray, p. 57).

The design argument from simple analogy can be stated in the form of an argument as follows:

1. The universe resembles a designed object just as the intelligent designs of human beings.
2. The design aspect of any human artifact is the

result of intelligent design.
3. Because like effects have like causes, the universe
was designed by an intelligent creator.

We can look at something as simple as a chair and know that it must have a designer. This is evident in the craftsmanship, the colors, and decorative fabric. It is obvious to the simplest observer that the chair did not evolve from a tree, or that it always existed and therefore does not require a designer. Since the universe exhibits these qualities of design, a high probability must exist that the universe has a designer.

This form of the design argument from simple analogy was expanded and refined by William Paley (1743 – 1805) in his well-known book *Natural Theology* (1802). Here, Paley makes the famous watchmaker argument by suggesting what one can infer when finding a watch on the ground.

> . . . *when we come to inspect the watch, we perceive. . . that its several parts are framed and put together for a purpose, e.g. that they are so formed and adjusted as to produce motion, and that motion so regulated as to point out the hour of the day; that if the different parts had been differently shaped from what they are, or placed after any other manner or in any other order than that in which they are placed, either no motion at all would have been carried on in the machine, or none which would have answered the use that is now served by it. . . . the inference we think is inevitable, that the watch must have had a maker --*

that there must have existed, at some time and at some place or other, an artificer or artificers who formed it for the purpose which we find it actually to answer, who comprehended its construction and designed its use (Paley, p. 112).

Paley's watchmaker argument has validity in how it shows that purpose in design can only come from an intelligent agent. In other words, many elements in the universe exhibit a functional complexity that serves a purpose. Like the watch, this purpose has meaning to the designer because it serves a highly specific purpose, with precise size, shape and parts that work together in harmony to perform this obvious purpose. Since the universe and nature have functional complexity, which only comes from a designer, then the universe and all of nature must also have a designer.

The Design Argument: Anthropic Principal

Another reason the first cause must be intelligent is based on our observation of the universe. The universe is a perfectly balanced machine. It has order and the appearance of design; but more than just the appearance - the universe functions as if designed. This is called the anthropic principal and applies to everything in the universe, from galaxies down to the smallest particle. The fundamental parameters of the universe appear to have been finely tuned to make life possible. According to Bernard Lovell (1913-2012),

English physicist and radio astronomer, everything in the universe is so exact, precise, and perfectly balanced that if the expansion rate at the moment of the big bang was off by one part in a thousand, million, millionths a second, the universe would have collapsed back onto itself and we would never have existed.

Another example, among many, of the anthropic principal is the gravitational force. If it were changed by more than 1 in 10^{40} we would not exist. Why is that number so exact? It had to be for life to exist. Should we assume this is mere chance, and naturalism made it all happen through unguided 'forces?' I think that would take a great deal of faith.

According to Arno Penzias (As quoted by Margenau, & Varghese, 1992), a Nobel Prize winner who helped to establish the big bang theory of cosmology:

"The universe was created out of nothing with exactly the right balance to permit life, and seems to have an almost supernatural plan."

Penzias is not suggesting that God exists; he is just unable to offer any other explanation that makes sense of the evidence. Fred Hoyle (1915-2001), the man who coined the term 'Big Bang', put it this way: *"It is as if a super-intellect has monkeyed with physics"*.

So are we to assume the perfect design of the universe happened naturally based on faith in naturalism? No, we should treat a natural explanation for the origin and precise balance of the universe with extreme skepticism.

Consciousness, Reason and Free Will

If we are to believe that all of humankind is a cosmic accident, and simply the result of material, time and chance, and exists only to propagate our DNA, then why do we have some of the attributes we have? For example, why do we have consciousness? How do raw nonliving materials evolve to consciousness? If our brains are merely chemical machines, how do we explain reason? Or trust our own reason? If we are just matter without a guided process, then our mind is just a mass of chemical reactions that should not be trusted any more than any other chemical reaction should be trusted for sound reason. Darwin had his own doubts about our ability to trust our capacity to reason (Gardner, 1999).

> "With me the horrid doubt always arises whether the convictions of man's mind, which has been developed from the mind of lower animals, are of any value or at all trustworthy. Would anyone trust in the convictions of a monkey's mind, if there are any convictions in such a mind?"
>
> -In a letter to William Graham, 1881.

Another important question is: do chemical reactions have free will? Do the chemicals fizzing in a beaker in some laboratory have the free will to decide anything? If naturalism and atheism are true, then our minds cannot possibly have free will. With such a mind, we cannot trust any of our thoughts, since our thoughts are purely chemical reactions and not reason.

Of course, we do have free will. There is no reason to believe that free will is an illusion, other than to lend support to the theory of naturalism. However, if we do not have free will, then how can we assume that our thoughts are our own, and not just a chemical reaction to the surrounding environment? In fact, if we do not have the free will to reason, then how can the atheist trust his own beliefs in atheism? Did he come to this conclusion through his own free will and reason?

The Final Burden of Proof

If you are like me, you did not become a Christian as a result of someone convincing you that God exists. I never doubted that. I did not need a logical argument to convince me. It has always been something deep in my being that seems self-evident. And this makes sense to me in light of what the Bible says:

> For his invisible attributes, namely, his eternal power and divine nature, have been clearly perceived, ever since the creation of the world, in the things that have been made. So they are without excuse.

> -Romans 1:20

According to this verse, we should know that God

exists without anyone convincing us. The very existence of the universe should be enough evidence! Of course, it is not enough for some people; because for some, there can never be enough. In this case, it may be a waste of time trying to convince someone that we have enough evidence to believe God exists, and that we can believe and remain rational at the same time.

The famous atheist philosopher Bertrand Russell (1872 - 1970) was asked what he would say to God if one day he is asked by God why he did not believe. He replied, "*Not enough evidence, God. Not enough evidence!*" This same view is still held by many atheists who demand evidence on the level of mathematical certainty for the existence of God. Yet these same atheists believe in many things that do not offer that level of evidence. In fact, very few things do.

As Christians, we must understand that a part of God's nature is his hidden attributes. That is, He does not reveal a physical and audible form of Himself to us today (as was the case with Jesus) that we can interact with naturally. We interact with God supernaturally, and that requires a measure of faith.

Because of God's hidden nature, we bear the burden of proof if we claim that God really exists. Obviously, no one can prove that God does not exist, but we (Christians) are making the claim that He does exist and we need to support that claim with evidence - and we can do that.

However, before we launch into a mound of evidence for God's existence, we should remind our atheist friends that they have a burden of proof also.

For example, to deny that God exists means that you must argue that life arose from non-life and the universe created itself, or was created spontaneously from nothing, or has existed forever. None of these things have been proven with mathematical certainty - and no one is even suggesting they have!

Many atheists will argue that we do not know what caused the universe to exist, but in time we will know through scientific means, and the cause will be natural. Of course, this is a huge assumption based on nothing more than a belief in naturalism - a belief that all there is in the universe is undirected natural forces. Of course, this is a philosophical position and not a scientific argument.

The atheist has even more to explain, such as, the assertion that the only way to discover the truth is through science. That is, without God, all we have is matter and motion in the universe. Christians have always believed that matter can be studied and truth found as a result. But, to argue that only science can discover truth is a self-defeating argument. How can the statement, "only science can discover the truth" be tested by science to see if it is true? What test can be conducted to confirm the statement's validity? The problem is, the assertion that only science can discover the truth cannot be tested by science, and therefore does not even meet its own standard for truth.

So what do you say to "not enough evidence?" First, you can agree that Christians do not have enough evidence to coerce anyone into believing. We do not have enough evidence for the existence of God to bully someone into agreeing with us. If someone wants to deny the existence of God, they will find a way.

Second, we need to remind atheists that they do not have enough evidence to coerce anyone into believing that atheism is true and life evolved from non-living chemicals. If life emerged from some unguided natural process, we should see it happening in nature on some level, but we do not. More importantly, the scientific community is not even arguing that we see it happening in nature. Even so, many believe that life from non-life is a confirmed fact. Of course, not all scientists believe this. Furthermore, there are many highly respected non-Christian scientists who dispute this "fact" and present powerful evidence to support their position. This can only mean that the evidence is far from watertight – and that is a fact! So keep that fact in mind when confronted with the "evidence" for a universe without God.

CHAPTER TWO

Darwin or Design

"For a man who does not believe in a miracle, a slow miracle would be just as incredible as a swift one."

-G.K. Chesterton

Obviously, science does not have answers to the biggest questions of life: the existence of God, the origin of the universe, and the origin of all life. Of course, when pressed on the issue of origins, the naturalists just say "we don't know yet." The atheist answer may also be presented in the form of un-provable theories, like multiple universes, or a general statement that implies "nature did it." In fact, it can be literally anything but God - because that is a non-natural cause.

Remember, the cosmological and design arguments are deductive arguments. This means they are based on known premises, just like any valid logical argument. You might not like the conclusion or agree with them, but that does not make the arguments non-rational. This is the broken record of atheism - that Christian theism is non-rational. But it's all very hypocritical when you consider that EVERY time an atheist cannot answer one of the big questions, they conclude that it cannot be God. This is the same error, in reverse, that atheists accuse Christians of committing.

Christians have long been accused of 'God of the gaps' arguments. Meaning, if we don't know the answer, we just insert God. Of course, this is a straw man argument, and does not characterize how Christians justify the existence of God. Even so, atheists make the very error they accuse Christians of making every time they plead 'Darwin of the Gaps.' If they don't know the answer, they assume it must be naturalism, even if the odds against it are overwhelming. Therefore, claiming there is a designer based on sound scientific reasoning is not a 'God of the gaps' argument. If atheists insist on exercising blind-faith in a chance-based Darwinian explanation that does not comport with current scientific evidence and observations, and is against all mathematical odds, that is their right. However, this should not be allowed to go unanswered when presented as the only path to reason.

Good scientific evidence does not mean absolute certainty - and never has. Therefore, belief in God is rational based on the many lines of evidence and the rational arguments for His existence. One of the major arguments comes from design; specifically, the argument that intelligent design is a better explanation of the observable evidence than Darwinism.

Should Christians Believe in Evolution?

Ever since Darwin published his book, *On the Origin of Species by Means of Natural Selection, or the Preservation of Favored Races in the Struggle for Life* (1859), Christians have responded in a number of ways. Over the years, the scope of responses has ranged from total outrage to full acceptance, and everything in between.

In 1925 the argument over evolution was brought to an apex in a court case formally titled *The State of Tennessee v. John Thomas Scopes*, now known simply as the Scopes Monkey Trail. In this case, John Scopes, a high school teacher, was accused of teaching evolution in a Tennessee public school in violation of Tennessee state law. Scopes was convicted and forced to pay a small fine, but the trial brought national attention to the question of what Christians should think about evolution.

Interestingly, the Scopes Monkey trial was not a battle between atheists and Christians, but between Christians represented by two different groups - the modernist and fundamentalists. This argument continues today in the Church between those who interpret scripture as teaching a young earth creationist model, and those who allow for some level of evolution driven by God's creative power.

So, should Christians believe in evolution? This is a difficult question when phrased in simple terms because we first have to define evolution so we can all agree on what we are claiming to believe. For example, many Christians believe in some aspects of Darwinism, such as survival of the fittest and natural selection. However, that does not translate into all life on Earth descending from a common primordial ancestor (common descent). Moreover, Darwinism is utterly insufficient to explain how the primordial ancestor arose from non-living chemicals.

To arrive at a definition, evolution must be subdivided into micro and macro. Microevolution explains the changes that occur over time within a specific species. On this level of evolution, natural selection results in dogs with thick fur in cold climates, and thin fur in hot climates. However, microevolution does not posit that either dog evolved from a fish. Microevolution can also be clearly seen in the outcomes of animal breeding. As a result, almost all Christians accept microevolution.

Macroevolution, on the other hand, is a very different theoretical framework. Macroevolution argues that microevolution, given enough time, resulted in the diversity of all life on earth arising from a single source. The Oxford Concise Science Dictionary defines macroevolution as:

The gradual process by which the present diversity of plant and animal life arose from the earliest and most primitive organisms, which is believed to have been continuing for the past 3000 million years.

This definition does not specify a single original primitive organism, but should because this is inevitable if macroevolution occurred through totally natural processes. The macroevolution view is held by some Christians who want to accept Darwinism and point to God as the catalyst who started the evolutionary process. In other words, God pushed the first domino and the rest is history. These theistic evolutionists, as they are known, only posit intelligent design and not a creation event as described in the Bible.

Another viewpoint comes from the progressive creationists, who believe that the earth is old, and possibly the universe, but the process of Darwinian evolution is not responsible for the diversity of all life on earth. In this more Biblical model, God created life much like we see it now, except for variations brought about by microevolution. For example, God could have created a single group of dogs; and since the creation event, dogs have interbred into the many variations we see today over thousands, or millions, of years. This view advocates the evidence for an old earth, and very old universe, which has been collected over the past 150 years. Progressive creationists do not interpret Genesis 1 as six literal, and total, days of creation.

The young earth creationists (YEC) are the group of Christians that believe in a 6000 – 10,000 year old earth and a young universe where God created everything in six literal days. Young earth creationists point to scripture as evidence that their model of creation is the most acceptable. There are two major organizations that work to provide evidence for the YEC model: The Institute for Creation Research and Answers in Genesis. Both of these organizations have collected mounds of evidence to support their view. However, creationism is not as easy to defend today as it was in years past due to the impossibility of publishing scholarly papers in major academic journals on the topic. On the other hand, Intelligent Design Theory (ID) is making great progress in demonstrating that all life is designed, and therefore must have a designer. ID theory has penetrated the academic community and is represented in major academic journals, and therefore able to reach the most vulnerable group – young college students.

When someone asks if you believe in evolution you should not assume they mean any of these Christian explanations of our origin. Why? Because in academia today the definition of evolution is totally Darwinian and totally godless. It is without any intelligent design or supernatural input. It is life from non-life through random, unguided, unintelligent mutations over millions of years. That is the definition in any public university and the same definition that is found in any K12 public school textbook. The definition of evolution never implies design or God.

Therefore, when evolution is discussed in academia it is a very specific version of the theory that does not accommodate ANY input that is not naturalistic or materialistic. So when Christians say they believe in evolution, they must qualify their statement and be able to explain which model they support. Christians are certainly free to believe in evolution, but not the 'textbook' version since it does not involve God. Christians have disagreed on Bible interpretation from the beginning, and the evolution debate is no different. This does not stop Christians from coming together to recognize that God created all life, including us, and give Him the glory He deserves.

For by him all things were created, in heaven and on earth, visible and invisible, whether thrones or dominions or rulers or authorities—all things were created through him and for him.

-Colossians 1:16

Intelligent Design

Intelligent Design is the science of seeking evidence of design in nature. ID Advocates argue that most features of the universe, and of life, are best explained by an intelligent cause and not undirected, random processes. Scientists can support this hypothesis by observing the types of information that results when intelligent agents act.

Intelligent Design theory has been tested using observational methods to detect design in the rapid origin of biological life, as in the Cambrian explosion where thousands of life forms appear suddenly in the geologic strata with no predecessors. This sudden appearance of life runs counter to the predictions of Darwin that postulated millions of years separating evolutionary stages of development. This slow development should be clearly visible in the fossil record, but none exist.

Intelligent Design is apparent in certain biological systems due to their inability to be 'reduced' and still function. This observation, called irreducible complexity, states that an irreducibly complex system is one that cannot function without any of its interrelating parts or elements. This can apply to something as simple as a mousetrap or a cilium (a common organelle found in eukaryotic cells), which cannot function without its microtubule-based cytoskeleton, molecular motor proteins, and tubulins. This leads to impossible questions for naturalists when larger irreducibly complex systems are considered. For example, how does an eye evolve when a half-evolved eye would not function as an eye, and therefore be eliminated by natural selection as a non-useful mutation? The answer is that an irreducibly complex system cannot be produced by slight changes over millions of years via biological evolution because each preceding version would be missing necessary un-evolved parts and therefore be non-functioning. The only reasonable explanation for irreducibly complex systems is that they arose suddenly by design with all parts already arranged and functioning.

One of the most exciting areas of research in ID is the discovery of biological information in cells. Pioneering work by Phillip Johnson (2010) and Stephen Meyer (2013) on the discovery of biological information in cells, particularly DNA and RNA, has the potential to change the debate on intelligent design and naturalism. It is possible that biological information will be the death of Darwinism within the next 20 to 30 years. As Dr. Meyer suggests, *"Neo-Darwinism and its associated theories of chemical evolution will not be able to survive the discoveries in biological information in the twenty first century"* (p. 34). Others have called the DNA molecule and its language of life the most efficient information processing system in the universe (Behe, 2006). As Bill Gates puts it, *"DNA is like a computer program but far, far more advanced than any software ever created"* (2008). With all the available evidence, DNA seems unlikely to have evolved through undirected chemical processes.

Unlike irreducible complexity, the argument from biological information challenges how life could have evolved from non-living matter before the "forces" of natural selection were present to direct evolution. The exact ordering of the four DNA nucleotides directs how proteins are constructed, which leads to the construction of cells. The ordering of these nucleotides can only be classified as information, which makes them just as unlikely to have evolved naturally as one of Shakespeare's plays. Meyer predicts the probability to be 1 in 10^{125}.

The primary issue at hand is that without

information already present to form the first protein strands and cells, life could not have started. Furthermore, natural selection cannot anticipate what form or function is needed for survival, only preserve the fittest already-living animals (Abel, 2010). Therefore, the information could not have created itself or decided what it should be to survive in the first place; it must have come from somewhere with that information already embedded.

The discovery of the information bearing properties of DNA and RNA is a major challenge to all naturalistic theories about the universe and the origins of biological life on Earth. This should not be surprising since the DNA code is a language made up of letters, representing the chemical sequence (A, T, G, and C), that spell out complex directions much like a computer program. Since there are only four characters, it can also be compared to the simple binary language that computers use to carry information (although DNA is more complex). The path of current research has the opportunity to demonstrate empirically that this information for life cannot be explained by naturalism.

Objections to ID

Some will argue that intelligent design is the same thing as creationism. Of course, it is not. ID is a process to experimentally detect whether the apparent design in nature is, in fact, the result of an intelligent agent. To keep the theory simple, there is no attempt to identify the source of the intelligent agent behind the design; the point is simply to establish genuine intelligent design.

There are some who have tried to argue there is no apparent design in nature, and therefore we should not look for an intelligent cause. However, this is a fringe view and not that of most trained biologists (atheist or not). For example, the most famous atheist in the world today is probably Richard Dawkins, who is a professor of biology at Oxford. Dawkins states in his book, *The Blind Watchmaker* (1986) that, "Biology is the study of complex things that appear designed for a purpose, but are just random accidents." Dawkins acknowledges the apparent design in nature, but prefers to interpret this as random accidents that, in reality, have an astronomically low probability of ever occurring.

Other attacks on ID typically try to denounce it as pseudoscience, or simply not science at all. Is this a fair assessment of ID? Of course not. Intelligent Design Theory follows the exact same scientific methodology that is standard in any public university research department. This is a four-step process that involves forming a hypothesis, making observations, conducting experiments, and drawing conclusions. The presupposition of ID (all scientific hypothesis have presuppositions) is that when intelligent agents act they produce complex and specified information (Dembski, 2011). Meaning, only a mind can produce information, and information only comes from a mind. We do not see information arise naturally in nature, under any circumstances, so why should we base our entire understanding of the origins of life on the assumption that it has already happened numerous times.

A common argument among naturalists to explain the apparent design of the universe is to posit multiple universes. Prominent atheist scientists, such as Stephen Hawking and Laurence Krauss, admit that our universe is unique and perfectly balanced for life on earth to exist. Brian Cox, advanced fellow in the School of Physics and Astronomy at the University of Manchester, has argued that we are most likely alone in the universe because the odds of life arising by chance only once is astronomically low, twice is virtually impossible. However, with multiple universe theory this does not pose a problem. After all, if an infinite number of universes exist, then it makes sense that one would be perfectly suited for life, right? It all makes sense until you ask for the evidence, which is non-existent. To argue that multiple universes exist based on a mathematical abstraction does not even rise to the level of circumstantial evidence. Furthermore, there is no actual evidence for multiple universes, and worse, no way to even test for them. To call this a serious scientific theory is laughable.

The Implications of ID

Christians only need to demonstrate one thing to defeat atheism: The intelligent design imbedded in all living things. If atheist argue that their view of the world is true, and everything evolved naturally, then the evidence must support the view. One way to refute the "evidence" for atheism is to consider the statistical odds of life arising from non-living chemicals. Since the probability of even a single protein randomly assembling is so astronomically small (DNA's sequence carries the code for making a protein), many scientists now prefer a new theory that suggest RNA molecules carried the first genetic information in its nucleotide sequence, and did not require DNA or proteins. Since this is a more basic process, some claim RNA to be the evolutionary predecessor to DNA.

However, the problem does not go away by theorizing that biological information arose naturally through RNA. For example, consider an RNA strand that is 300 nucleotides long (they can be 7000 nucleotides long). Each nucleotide in the sequence can be either an A, C, G or U. Therefore, the possibility of the correct RNA strand randomly assembling is 4^{300}. This number is more than astronomically large. There is not enough time for it to have happened by random chance even once in 13 billion years, which is the accepted age of the universe.

Some atheists will argue that lab experiments under controlled conditions will yield random results that mimic the evolution of RNA. There is a huge problem with this line of thinking, which is, I could just as easily conduct an experiment in the lab and manage the conditions so that the apparent evolution of RNA never happens, and then claim this is what occurs with 'random' results.

Let's consider the facts that are widely agreed upon:

It is estimated that there are 10^{80} atoms in the universe. Each atom has 10^{45} possible random interactions per second. Based on the age of the universe, there have been approximately 10^{150} total possible, random, purposeless, natural events that have taken place in order for the first cell to evolve by chance. As a result, some scientists have placed the odds of the simplest cell evolving by chance at 1 in 10^{3000} (Deamer, 2009). If these estimates are even roughly accurate, then belief in life arising from non-life by chance is on par with science fiction/fantasy. It is not science; it is a philosophical presupposition that, unfortunately, guides all thinking for the origin of life in public universities.

Suppose we take these odds and use them logically to argue for God's existence. It would work like this: let's use Aristotle's law of the excluded middle. It states that for any proposition, either that proposition is true, or its negation is true. In this case, life either evolved from non-living chemicals or it did not. There is no third option - that much is agreed upon. So if life did not evolve from non-life, then it was created. Again, there is no third option. Therefore, if the odds against the first cell arising from non-living material without a designer is 1 in 10^{3000}, then its negation, the odds FOR a designer, is essentially certain.

These odds in favor of a designer are perfectly rational, because they are deductions based on what we know. Furthermore, evolutionary scientists cannot even begin to answer a few simple questions about the origin of life. They are:

(1) How can life arise from non-living materials
- randomly or not?
(2) How can highly complex (DNA)
information evolve without a prior intelligence
to design the information?
(3) How can information come from a purely
material universe?

In fact, no one anywhere can answer these
questions, no matter what anyone has to say on the
subject. Here is the proof: Professor James M. Tour of
Rice University, one of the ten most cited chemists in
the world, said this about life evolving from non-living
chemicals:

*"...I simply do not understand, chemically, how
macroevolution could have happened.... Does
anyone understand the chemical details behind
macroevolution? If so, I would like to sit with that
person and be taught, so I invite them to meet with
me."*

In a speech at Georgia Tech, Dr. Tour said this:

*"I was once brought in by the Dean of the
Department, many years ago, and he was a chemist.
He was kind of concerned about some things. I said,
"Let me ask you something. You're a chemist. Do you
understand this? How do you get DNA without a
cell membrane? And how do you get a cell membrane*

without a DNA? And how does all this come together from this piece of jelly?" We have no idea, we have no idea. I said, "Isn't it interesting that you, the Dean of science, and I, the chemistry professor, can talk about this quietly in your office, but we can't go out there and talk about this?"

Dr. Tour has made it clear that no scientist that he has spoken with – not even Nobel Prize winners - understands how dead chemicals bonded together and made the first life forms. In fact, Tour joined 900 other scientists to sign a document called *A Scientific Dissent from Darwinism*. This document states, *"We are Skeptical of claims for the ability of random mutation and natural selection to account for the complexity of life. Careful examination of the evidence for Darwinian Theory should be encouraged."*

So don't be impressed by highly intelligent professors working in a lab under highly controlled, non-chance conditions to prove that life arose by chance. The probability of this EVER happening via unguided natural means is astronomically low. If life did arise on this planet by totally natural, unguided evolutionary means, then it is literally a miracle - and therefore evidence for the existence of God!

The Fossil Record

If you ask for evidence for Darwinian evolution, you will likely be presented with the most common evidence given: the fossil record. There is no discussion of Darwinian evolution that does not include the bones of ancient animals in the geologic column. Every textbook on the subject of Darwin goes into great detail about the fossil record as an evolutionary moving picture that demonstrates the origin of the spectacular diversity of all life on Earth. Every public school child is presented with a fossil record that supports the claim that the origin of all life is unguided, natural, and without any input from an intelligent agent. In reality, the fossil record supports none of these things.

The fossil record has been a problem for Darwinism from the beginning. Even before publishing *The Origin of Species* in 1859, Darwin had his own reservations about the ability to use the fossil record as evidence for the common descent of all life from a single primordial source. This is because Darwin's theory depends on very small changes over long periods of time which gradually changes one species into a totally different species, but the fossil records do not support the theory. If very slow changes occurred over millions of years, then billions of fossils of the intermediate species would exist in the geologic record. It turns out, they do not. Darwin readily admitted this fact:

> *"Why then is not every geological formation and every strata full of such intermediate links? Geology assuredly does not reveal any such finely-graduated organic chain; and this perhaps, is the most obvious and serious objection which can be urged against my theory."*
>
> – Charles Darwin, Origin of the Species

One wonders why, if Darwin knew this, he would continue pushing this theory the rest of his life. Darwin pointed to the lack of evidence in the global fossil record for his theory, but assumed that more transitional forms of the various species would be found as the research progressed. However, it's been 155 years and the fossil record has yet to produce the evidence that supports Darwin's theory. This is not an opinion of Christian apologists, this is a fact readily admitted by modern evolutionary biologist.

> *"The Cambrian strata of rocks, vintage about 600 million years, are the oldest in which we find most of the major invertebrate groups. And we find many of them already in an advanced state of evolution, the very first time they appear. It is as though they were just planted there, without any evolutionary history. Needless to say, this appearance of sudden planting has delighted creationists"*
> - Richard Dawkins, The Blind Watchmaker

Again we find Dawkins arguing that the evidence supports design, but we should ignore it. The Cambrian strata that Dawkins is referring to is a layer of rock dated at approx. 600 million years where a large variety of ancient life can be found. These fossils appear suddenly in the geologic record as if they popped out of thin air. The appearance of so many fossils in one area of the strata is so remarkable it's called the Cambrian explosion by scientists; yet science has no empirical method to explain the sudden appearance of so many fossils at once. As stated by Dembski (2006), *"Almost all cases of the Cambrian animals have no clear morphological antecedents in earlier Vendian or Precambrian fauna"* (p. 177). This means that animals appeared in the fossil record with no evidence of earlier ancestral species, as Darwinism would require. Darwin agreed:

> *"To the question why we do not find rich fossiliferous deposits belonging to these assumed earliest periods prior to the Cambrian system I can give no satisfactory answer . . . Nevertheless, the difficulty of assigning any good reason for the absence of vast piles of strata rich in fossils beneath the Cambrian system is very great.*
>
> -The Origin of Species

Another reason Darwin continued to promote his unsupported theory of common descent was because he and other scientists of his day assumed that the precursors to the Cambrian species were soft body animals and therefore would not fossilize very well, therefore explaining their absence in the pre-Cambrian geologic layers. However, in 2010 paleontologists found more than 1,500 soft-bodied marine animal fossils believed to date back 500 million years (Van Roy et.al, 2010). To date, many examples of soft-bodied animals have been found in the fossil record all over the world. None explain where the Cambrian fossils came from or provide the intermediate data needed to support Darwin's theory.

It should be clear to anyone taking a cursory look at the fossil record that it does not support common decent of all species from a single ancestor. Darwinism, and the modern definition of macroevolution, not only depends on this to be true, but proclaims it from every rooftop as fact. This proclamation is made as if everyone in the scientific community wholeheartedly agrees, but this is far from the truth. For example, Dr. Colin Patterson, Senior Paleontologist at the British Museum says:

> *"As a paleontologist myself, I am much occupied with the philosophical problems of identifying ancestral forms in the fossil record. You say that I should at least "show a photo of the fossil from which each type of organism was derived." I will lay it on the line - there is not one such fossil for which one could make a watertight argument."*

Dr. Colin is joined by other scientists who, despite their belief in macroevolution, honestly admit that the fossil record does not provide the evidence necessary to demonstrate common decent. Other examples of this candor follow.

> *"Despite the bright promise that paleontology provides a means of "seeing" evolution, it has presented some nasty difficulties for evolutionists, the most notorious of which is the presence of "gaps"*

in the fossil record. Evolution requires intermediate forms between species and paleontology does not provide them..."

-David B. Kitts. PhD (Zoology), Head Curator of the Department of Geology at the Stoval Museum

"My attempts to demonstrate evolution by an experiment carried on for more than 40 years have completely failed... The fossil material is now so complete that it has been possible to construct new classes, and the lack of transitional series cannot be explained as being due to scarcity of material. The deficiencies are real, they will never be filled."

-N. Heribert Nilsson, botanist, evolutionist and professor at Lund University in Sweden

"No fossil is buried with its birth certificate. That, and the scarcity of fossils, means that it is effectively impossible to link fossils into chains of cause and effect in any valid way... To take a line of fossils and claim that they represent a lineage is not a scientific hypothesis that can be tested, but an assertion that carries the same validity as a bedtime story — amusing, perhaps even instructive, but not scientific."

-Dr. Henry Gee, a British paleontologist and evolutionary biologist.

"All paleontologists know that the fossil record contains precious little in the way of intermediate forms; transitions between major groups are characteristically abrupt."

-Stephen Jay Gould, World Renown Professor of Geology and Paleontology, Harvard

Gould's comments are significant since he is the scientist who aspired to solve the gaps in the fossil record with a new theory he called *Punctuated Equilibrium* (1972). This theory presumably solves the problem with gaps in the fossil record by assuming they should not be there in the first place. Punctuated equilibrium posits that evolution occurs mainly in sudden bursts, with long periods of little change in between. This explains why transitional fossils cannot be found.

There are more than a few problems with Gould's theory of punctuated equilibrium worth noting. First, if species change can happen in short evolutionary bursts, then why can't we see it in nature? We are told repeatedly by Darwinists that we cannot see the process of evolution because it takes millions of years and the changes are gradual. But if the changes are now assumed to be punctuated, then we should see some evidence for the theory in nature – other than gaps in the fossil record.

Second, punctuated equilibrium can be described as an ad hoc explanation. In other words, it seems that the theory was adopted because it fits a Darwinists view of the fossil record, not because there is any evidence for it. In fact, the evidence for punctuated equilibrium is the lack of evidence in the fossil record. This is like saying you have evidence that your neighbor broke into your house based on the lack of evidence that your neighbor broke into your house. This does not work in real life, and it is not sufficient for scientific discovery.

Conclusion

So now we return to the question: is it Darwin or design? It's clear that a lot of people want it to be Darwin, despite the evidence. If only science could just tell us the truth. Unfortunately, science does not tell us anything - scientists do. Data is interpreted while looking through the lens of personal worldview, biases, and presuppositions. Although that is true for both sides in this argument, the evidence cannot be ignored. If Darwinism is true, and all life on earth came from a natural source with no input from an intelligent agent, then why does biological life look designed, function as if designed, and carry information at its core? On the other hand, if God exists then we should see signs of His design in all life and poor evidence for a purely natural origin. This is what we see. Many Atheists even agree that this is what we see. So maybe the most obvious explanation is true.

McLeod

CHAPTER THREE

The Moral Argument

"Whenever you find a man who says he doesn't believe in a real Right and Wrong, you will find the same man going back on this a moment later."

— C.S. Lewis

As a Christian, one of the most powerful arguments you have for the existence of God is the moral argument. This argument strikes at the heart of every human being, because to be human is to recognize moral truths and moral duties. The moral argument for the existence of God shows us that we have a nonmaterial author of unchanging morality. The existence of a universal moral law is just as factual as the existence of the universe. God created both for mankind to live in and live by. Unlike the cosmological and design arguments, the moral argument is not based on empirical scientific evidence but is a philosophical and nonmaterial factor of human existence. The logical argument can be expressed as follows:

1. If God does not exist, objective moral values do not exist.
2. Objective moral values do exist.
3. Therefore, God exists.

The fact that moral laws and moral duties exist is unequivocal. Every person (apart from the mentally ill) in every country in the world believes that certain things are wrong, such as harming children for fun. These things are not wrong because they are frowned upon by society, or illegal, but because they are objectively wrong. Ultimate right and wrong is not subjective, like your opinion about a flavor of ice cream or favorite movie. Objective right and wrong is written on the heart of every person and comes from outside of human jurisdiction – otherwise, right and wrong would be totally subjective.

Without God as the ultimate law giver, objective morality cannot exist, because it would simply be a man-made construct and subject to change based on situational forces. Therefore, atheists should be comfortable with this concept – but they are not. Only the most honest atheist will concede that without God, moral laws and duties have no objective meaning. Some well-known atheist philosophers have adopted this position, called moral relativism; yet, most of them failed to live by the philosophy. For example, the aforementioned Bertrand Russell argued that moral absolutes do not exist, but protested the war in Europe. Why? What made the war wrong if right and wrong do not exist? Russell may not have liked the war, but that was just his opinion. It was, by no means, objectively wrong if moral absolutes do not exist. Someone else may have liked the war; so for that person, the war was good if right and wrong are subjective.

On the flip side of this coin, most atheists will argue that God does not exist (due to lack of evidence) but absolute moral duties do. But where do these absolute moral duties come from? What evidence suggests they exist? Can we conduct an empirical experiment to prove they exist?

If atheism is true, and nothing supernatural exists, then only the natural and material exist. This means that non-material things, such as morals, do not really exist.

To argue that we need an empirical level of evidence for the existence of God but not for the existence of moral absolutes is a serious contradiction. This is what Francis Shaffer (1912-1984) referred to as atheists living in a two story house. They live on the first floor where God does not exist, and then leap to the second floor where God does exist when objective morality is needed.

Therefore, to throw out objective morality is to throw out absolute moral facts. When the atheist does this, he gives up his right to say something is right or wrong. A true right and wrong only makes sense if we agree that a standard exists outside of ourselves. To say that "rape is wrong," or "the murder of children is wrong" is just hollow words and an expression of opinion. They are simply likes and dislikes. If we reduced morality to likes and dislikes, then we are worse than animals.

It's important to start a discussion on absolute right and wrong and absolute moral duties by understanding that without something unmovable, untouchable, and uncorrupted by human beings, we cannot claim that such a thing as objective moral law really exists. What follows in this chapter are the various consequences and contradictions of a world without a moral law giver.

Can we be good without God?

Most Atheists make the claim that we can live good moral lives without believing in God, and most Christians would agree with this statement; probably because most Christians know someone who is an atheist that lives a good moral life.

But the real question is whether atheism can provide a justification for morality. Many atheists today do not like to argue that morality is relative, since that philosophy leads down a very dark path. Let's face it, without an objective moral law, there is no right or wrong – and that is a very dark prospect. Furthermore, it's hard to argue that right and wrong are just someone's opinion and totally subjective, like a flavor of ice cream or a favorite movie.

As a result, some prominent atheists have argued that morality just "is", while others, like Richard Dawkins, argue that morality is a necessity of evolution to enable us to further our reproductive ends. Still others call morality an evolutionary illusion.

But each of these views fails to provide justification for an objective right and wrong – the kind of right and wrong that is true no matter who agrees or disagrees with it.

It should be obvious to any thinking person that without God to ground right and wrong, it's just your opinion, or the community's opinion, or the government's opinion, or even more likely – the person with the biggest gun's opinion.

In other words, if morality has nothing to do with God, what does it have to do with? If morality is relative, and just an individual matter, then who can say that a serial killer like Ted Bundy is wrong. If it's up to the individual culture, or the state, then who can say the Nazis were wrong? You may not like what Hitler did, and you probably would not do what Hitler did, but that's just your opinion if an objective right and wrong does not exist.

If there is nothing unmovable and outside the reach of human beings to pin objective morality on, then who's to say what's right and wrong. Me? You? The state? The world? Just think of the consequences of each of those choices.

There are consequences because, without an objective standard, we do not all agree on what good or bad means. As stated, I think most atheists are good moral people, and I think most Christians who know an atheist believe this claim. But I would like to question that assertion for a moment.

Sure, atheists seem to behave as well as any other citizen. That is, they behave in a way that adheres to the same moral law of society as Christians – for the most part. Of course, we are talking about the big issues here: robbery, murder, rape, torture …etc.

However, when you know that another person is not morally tied to objective right and wrong because of a belief in God, then how can you ever predict their behavior in a given situation? If God does not exist and is not looking over the shoulder of the atheist, then how can anyone be sure that the atheist will always respond in a given manner? Sure, Christians often fail to respond in the way commanded by Christian doctrine; but we can appeal to the Christian's belief in an objective moral law. How do we do that with an atheist? Maybe we cannot. The truth is, the atheist's worldview allows for situational ethics and a morality based on what is best for the atheist. After all, that's just evolution and natural selection at work.

Nevertheless, there are well-known atheists who attempt to argue for an objective, or empirically based, system of morality that makes no reference to God. *Act utilitarianism* is one such theory which argues that an action is objectively moral if it causes more good than harm. Some define it as an act that produces more pleasure than pain. A popular example used by utilitarians is to consider the act of watching TV all day or going down to the local homeless shelter and volunteering. Between these two choices, helping at the homeless shelter is the morally right thing to do because it does more good than watching TV. Although this may be true, there are some glaring problems with this philosophy.

First, who decides what is good? In some cases it is obvious, but in other cases it's not so clear. Which, of course, leads us back to the same problem. One person may think that more good is produced by making as much money as possible at the expense of everything else. This case could be made based on the fact that the money could be used for charity. But what about the individuals family? Or health? Both of these are known to suffer when the pursuit of money is the main goal. Other scenarios are easy to dream up, but why not a real-life example of how this atheist morality looks in practice.

Richard Dawkins is fond of arguing that morality is what increases the sum of happiness and results in the least suffering. Obviously Dawkins is a proponent of Act utilitarianism. Not long Ago, Dawkins came under fire for a post on Twitter where he said that Down syndrome babies should be aborted. In the face of a storm of criticism for his comment, Dawkins tweeted:

"Given a free choice of having an early abortion or deliberately bringing a Down child into the world, I think the moral and sensible choice would be to abort...I personally would go further and say that, if your morality is based, as mine is, on a desire to

increase the sum of happiness and reduce suffering, the decision to deliberately give birth to a Down baby, when you have the choice to abort it early in the pregnancy, might actually be immoral from the point of view of the child's own welfare....Having said that, the choice would be entirely yours and I would never dream of trying to impose my views on you or anyone else."

Dawkins, and others like him, who want to give up God and keep objective morality are facing a difficult contradiction. On the one hand, he says that the "choice to abort" is the moral thing to do. However, in the next sentence he admits that it does not matter what someone actually does in this case and he cannot make a judgment call. Why? If Dawkins' form of morality is so weak that he cannot even stand by it in the wake of criticism, then what good is it? Does he really believe anything he says? Will his opinion simply change tomorrow after more criticism?

I'm not arguing that all atheists are immoral, because that's not true. I'm arguing that the atheist cannot rationalize their grip on a moral standard, and therefore, are free to abandon it if they so choose. In other words, they can change their idea of what 'good' means over time, if that is needed for progress, survival, or whatever.

It's true that atheists recognize that some things are just right and some things are just wrong. But using evolution, natural selection and the propagation of our genes as the reason for moral duties falls short of convincing. Why? Because if we are evolving animals who survive only when strong and best able to pass on our genetic material to offspring, then why develop altruism, kindness, compassion, love? Why not just step all over anyone who gets in your way and take everything you can from everyone else for your own survival? Because, the objective morality written on our hearts by God is not just for survival. It is there so we can live as we were created - in the image of God. According to the Bible, atheists also know this and it explains why they live as if an objective moral law exists.

> *For when Gentiles, who do not have the law, by nature do what the law requires, they are a law to themselves, even though they do not have the law. They show that the work of the law is written on their hearts, while their conscience also bears witness, and their conflicting thoughts accuse or even excuse them.*
>
> -Romans 2:14-15

So, can we be good without God? Yes, but without God, good has no meaning.

Moral Relativism

Some atheists argue that objective moral standards do exist. Moral standards can be defined as moral values (is something good or bad) and moral duties (moral obligation, what you should or should not do).

Of course, these arguments do a poor job of explaining how this is possible without God. At best, atheists have only given a possible explanation that argues we act the way we do in order to hold society together. However, this does not make moral duties objective in any way. As pointed out, this philosophy of moral duties is subject to change when society deems it necessary for survival. Therefore, with this logic, moral duties are totally subjective.

The moral relativist, on the other hand, is a more realistic atheist who understands that, without God, objective moral values and duties do not exist. To the moral relativist, right and wrong are individual or community choices. With this worldview, an action can be right for me, but wrong for you at the same time and in the same sense. This applies to rape, murder, or any other act you can think of that is obviously wrong. To the moral relativist, moral laws and duties are not transcendent, and therefore do not collectively apply to all people at all times.

Moral relativism is very fashionable on the college campus. Many college students will applaud the concept of subjective right and wrong. Some like the idea because they realize it lets them off the hook for sin. Others accept it as a rational consequence of a universe without God. Still others blather on about it without much understanding of the real consequences or contradictions of their position. Meaning, they claim to believe in moral relativism only until faced with a moral truth they are passionate about.

A good illustration of how moral relativists have

influenced the college campus can be found in an article I recently came across by a fellow apologist (Lenny Esposito). A student at a Christian university gave a presentation on the morality of embryonic stem-cell research. In the presentation, the student argued that destroying an embryonic stem-cell is the same as destroying a human being and is therefore wrong. At the end of the presentation the student was asked to explain why it was wrong. She explained that it was wrong for her, but she could not impose her moral view on someone else who may want to fund embryonic stem-cell research. Therefore, this student attending a Christian university held a moral relativists position, which is something totally opposed to Christian theology. Unfortunately, this is becoming more common at Christian universities around the country.

I once asked an atheist student of mine to explain to me how, if God does not exist, anyone can say that torturing children for fun is objectively wrong. He answered, "Well, I can't say that it's wrong." Needless to say, I was shocked. I know that this student would not torture a child for any reason, but since he had bought into moral relativism, he could not bring himself to say that something is wrong. The problem with both of these students is they respond to moral questions in relative terms, but live their lives as though objective moral values exist. There is an obvious problem with their worldview.

The problems with moral relativism are many. First, moral relativism is a denial that right and wrong come from an absolute source. But if no absolute source exists for right and wrong, then where do we get this concept? If not from God, then from where?

Does it come from nature? Many atheists make this claim, but how can a genuine right and wrong come from undirected matter? How can dead chemicals rearrange themselves into living matter, via natural selection and random processes, and then develop objective moral duties that we should follow? This seems incoherent.

Do morals come from something in me? Does the individual just decide what is right and wrong? If so, this would lead to the problem that what is right for me may be wrong for you. This is fine if we are talking about a career choice, or a genre of music, but not rape and murder.

Do morals come from society? Moral relativists propose that morality is just a social construct developed through evolution to enable humans to live together in communities, cooperate, and propagate the species. This is a reasonable argument, but flawed in that we can only expect subjective morals duties to arise from this source. After all, if society is free to decide what is right and wrong, then society is free to change its mind. What is objective about this? Also, one nation cannot charge another with human rights violations, since objective human rights would come from the state in the first place.

Some argue that right and wrong come from world consensus. But for this to be true, we must believe that getting more people to agree with you turns a subjective truth into an objective one. That cannot happen. An objective truth is true no matter who agrees or disagrees – or how many people are on each side of the issue.

Therefore, we are left with only one reasonable conclusion: moral absolutes come from God. Without God, moral absolutes cannot exist. This is a package deal; you cannot have one without the other. So when atheists argue that some things are just 'right' and some things are just 'wrong,' they are living in contradiction with their own worldview.

Based on the previous argument, it seems clear that morality without God is moral relativism. This is clear because human beings do not determine right and wrong, human beings discover right and wrong. The problem is, once discovered, human beings cannot agree on where they found right and wrong.

To further demonstrate the problems of moral relativism, we need only look at some of its most basic flaws. There are many, but I will just name a few. First, Moral law is self-evident. This can be demonstrated in the fact that no one can make a reasonable argument claiming that torturing children for fun is OK. Under no circumstances, in any place, at any time, would this be OK. This is a self-evident truth that resides in the hearts of all sane people. Therefore, this proves that moral absolutes do exist. This alone defeats the concept of moral relativism.

Another serious flaw of moral relativism is that moral relativists cannot blame others for harm caused to them, or even accept praise for something they did that was good. How can the moral relativist complain when someone steals his car? Of course he does not like this, but to say that it's wrong is incoherent in a world where right and wrong does not exist. It may not have been wrong for the car thief. Who is to say?

By the same logic, how can the moral relativist accept praise, when praise is a moral judgment? Why should anyone tell a moral relativist that she did something good? 'Good' is a moral judgment and the moral relativist does not believe in moral judgments – especially from Christians.

How can someone who denies that objective right and wrong exist claim anything is unfair or unjust? Again, it does not make sense to deny that God exists, and as a consequence moral absolutes do not exist, but then protest corrupt government, war, or Wall Street greed. The moral relativist may not like these things, but to say they are wrong is just not consistent with the relativist's worldview.

So, it should be obvious that it's difficult to be a true practicing moral relativist. Some very well-known atheist philosophers have done that, but they are the exception. In reality, very few people can claim that moral duties are relative and live their lives as though it's true. Sure, many people may claim this philosophy, but do they really live it?

Just for fun, assume you want to hire someone to paint your house, and you hire a moral relativist (because he is out of work and you can get a good price). You both agree on a fair price for the work and when the work should be done. You insist that he must be on time at 5am the next morning. He comes to your house the next morning at 5am with all of his painting equipment and ready to do the job, but when he gets out of his work truck, you tell him:

"I've decided to fire you from this job, I don't like Ford trucks, and you drive a Ford truck."

"What does that have to do with anything? We had an agreement!"

"Yes, we had an agreement, but I don't want to honor it now."

"You can't do that, I got up at 4am this morning and gathered all my equipment to be here on time. This is not right!"

"Wait, I thought you said you were a moral relativist?

"Yes, that's right."

"And moral relativist claim there is no objective right and wrong, and morality is totally subjective."

"Yes, but…"

"Then my personal morality tells me not to let you paint my house because I don't like your truck. That seems right to me."

Treating someone this way is obviously wrong by any standard, and we know this because we all have God's ultimate standard written on our hearts. Anyone can claim that a moral standard is an illusion, and there is no such thing as right or wrong or an ultimate standard of justice - until someone treats them unjustly. Furthermore, moral relativists rail against injustice as much as any other group. But how can relativists demand justice when they do not recognize a moral standard for justice? The moral argument for the existence of God is supported by a single underlining basic moral truth that all people understand, whether they recognize the author of the law or not.

The Problem of Evil

In virtually every debate between atheists and Christians, the issue of evil is used to deny the existence of God. This is argued based on the logic that God and evil cannot co-exist, and since it's obvious that evil does exist - then God must not.

Unlike most of the world's religions, Christianity accounts for the presence of suffering in the world and never denies that evil exists. The Bible teaches that God created man in His own image and gave humankind the opportunity to choose good over evil. For this to be true, human beings must be able to choose evil as well as good. Unfortunately, these choices have consequences that affect everyone, even the innocent.

On the other hand, if human beings could not choose to do evil, then how could they choose to do good? Without free will, we are no different from a doll that says "I love you" when the string is pulled. If that is all human beings are, then no one could actually choose God.

Before the Atheist can eliminate God because of evil and suffering, he has some difficult questions to answer. First, does evil even exist without God? If God does not exist, then who can say what is evil? Isn't the suffering in the world just natural selection running its course? Atheists want to label things they don't like as evil, but does evil really exist in a naturalistic world where only matter and motion exist? It's just nature, you can't call it evil or good, it just is.

Second, can a world without evil even exist? After all, without evil, how would we know what is good? As C.S. Lewis said, *"A man does not call a line crooked unless he has some idea of a straight line. What was I comparing this universe with when I called it unjust?"* Would we even have the concept of good? Is such a world even possible?

And finally, when will atheists start asking: Why is there good in the world? Why would love, honesty, kindness, sacrifice, and courage exist without God?

For some reason, atheists assume that we live in a naturally good world that has been contaminated by evil, as if a world naturally evolving by unintelligent, un-directed, non-personal forces would automatically evolve into a good world. That is a highly speculative assumption and it does not logically follow from natural evolution.

Yes, the problem of evil and suffering is a serious issue and you will likely be confronted by this problem as a Christian. Recently, I discussed this with an atheist who called in to a radio program I was hosting. He told me that he did not believe in God because of the suffering in the world. He could not believe that a loving God would allow such suffering. Therefore, in his mind, God must not exist. Interestingly, he told me he believed in right and wrong. I pointed out that his atheist worldview does not allow for an objective right and wrong, therefore he should not claim these things exist. The moment you give up God, you give up the right to talk about objective evil. Also, I pointed out that God can co-exist with evil. There is no automatic reason to conclude that God cannot. God can allow free will, and as a result human evil, without intervening to stop it based on His own reasons.

Atheists are quick to point out that there cannot possibly be a reason to allow such evil, but that's a bit presumptuous because it makes the assumption that we can understand all of God's motives and know everything that God knows. If that were the case, we would be just like God – and we are not.

It is also the height of presumption to assume that something we don't like, such as suffering in the world, means God does not exist. Using this logic, you could deny God's existence based on spinach. One may argue, "*I don't like spinach! If God exists, then He created spinach. Therefore I do not believe in a God that would make something I dislike so much.*"

Evil is a very common reason given for the denial of God's existence, but not a sufficient reason to deny that God exists. Although I have given rational arguments here, I do not want to downplay the issue of faith. When evil and suffering reaches our own doorstep, no rational argument will provide sufficient comfort. It is more likely that faith in God will be the best comfort available to those who suffer.

Conclusion

I have tried to show how God and moral meaning cannot be separated. Yes, atheists can claim that God is not needed to live a good life – and this is true. A popular atheist billboard says, "There is no God, so be good for goodness sake." The problem, as you now know, is that atheists cannot define 'good' outside of their own opinions.

Obviously, when we eliminate God we forfeit absolute moral law, but it's even worse than that. Without God, the alternative is very disturbing - a life where our very existence is ultimately meaningless. In this reality one can live as Mother Teresa or Adolf Hitler, and in the end, it will make no difference. Without God, the evil will never be punished and the good will never be rewarded. In the end, the universe will fall victim to the same cosmic forces that vomited up humanity by random chance. The sun will eventually burn out, all the energy in the universe will be depleted, and all the cosmos will return to nothing but the cold blackness of space. At that moment, how we lived our lives will have no meaning. Only with God can ultimate meaning be given to anything we do while we live; and only with God can ultimate hope exist after we die.

McLeod

CHAPTER FOUR

Why Jesus?

"Christianity, if false, is of no importance, and if true, of infinite importance. The only thing it cannot be is moderately important."

-C. S. Lewis

Once we get past the arguments for God's existence, the next question is: Who is God? Among non-Christians, the God-believers outnumber atheists by a wide margin. In other words, there are a lot of people who believe in God – of some kind – but are not convinced that Jesus is the manifestation of God or the only way to heaven. This is particularly true today where pluralism (all paths lead to God) is commonly accepted, especially among young people.

Like most Christians, I've been asked many times why I think that Christianity is the only true religion. In a world full of religions, literally thousands, how do we know that Christianity represents the real truth that identifies the real God? Billions of people follow different teachings such as Judaism, Islam, Hinduism, Buddhism, new age teachings, and many other minor religions. Are they all doomed? Can all these religions be false while Christianity remains uniquely true? Even if Christianity is true, why is it the only religion that leads to God? Don't other religions have the same ability to lead one to God just like Christianity? Other religions promote peace and goodness just like Christianity, so how can they all be wrong?

These are difficult questions and, no doubt, questions that can confront you in a culture where tolerance means accepting all religions as equally true. After all, how do you make a convincing argument that Christianity is true and all other world religions are wrong? Where do you even begin?

Although Christianity shares many beliefs with other religions, such as the belief in a personal creator of the universe who is the source of moral law and who holds us accountable, there are a couple of key differences. First, Christianity offers historical evidence with eyewitness testimony that supports the claim that Jesus rose from the grave. Second, and very important in a comparison of religions, Christianity can be falsified. That is, unlike any other religion in the world that makes claims about the identity of God, Christianity can actually be proven wrong – this makes it a credible assertion. Think about it; if I make a claim that no one can prove wrong, then why even try to investigate the claim. The claim has no possibility of being proven right or wrong – it is worthless as an argument. But with Christianity, all you have to do is show good evidence that Jesus did not rise from the grave and all the other claims of Christians are defeated.

In Jesus, we have good historical evidence to believe that He claimed to be the absolute manifestation of God - and he proved it by rising from the grave! The evidence for this claim, presented in the next chapter, is truly remarkable.

Other Worldviews

Human beings interpret the world via their worldview. As a consequence, worldviews are directly tied to beliefs about the big questions; and of course, the big questions are typically answered by one's religious views - or lack thereof. Although faith is a major factor in choosing one's religious views, reason should not be excluded. The rational person has determined that truth is not an abstract concept, but instead realizes that truth is what best describes and corresponds with reality. The rational mind also accepts, through logical consistency, that truth is knowable. Therefore, we can separate truth from fantasy when dealing with the question of worldviews.

Although there are many religions, there are only three primary religious worldviews, and each has its own way of viewing reality. They are: atheism, pantheism, and theism.

Atheism - In general terms, atheism is a worldview that presupposes a material-only universe. The new atheists boast that rationality is on their side because they only accept a reality that is material. In other words, there is no 'super' natural, or anything outside of nature. However, this worldview has crashed into the brick wall that Christianity predicted it would. Without God, humankind has no basis for objective truth, objective morality, human consciousness, logic, the concept of beauty, the appreciation of art, and many other things that are obviously non-material. As a result, atheists do not have a solid foundation for all truth because their worldview forces them to see only a narrow reality. This is a material-only reality.

Christians do not have this problem because their worldview is much more encompassing of reality. Christians consider science in all its technical wonder, as well as the non-material. As a result, Christianity explains the whole of reality better than atheism.

Pantheism - Most pantheists believe that the universe and everything in it is God, including mankind, and that the universe has existed forever, uncaused and uncreated. Therefore, pantheists do not believe in a personal creator God that is involved in the lives of people. Although many forms of pantheism are practiced around the world today, the main themes found in all forms are the all-encompassing unity of the material universe and the holiness of nature. Hinduism, Shintoism, Taoism, Jainism, and Buddhism are examples of pantheist religions and make up about 30% of the world's population.

Theism - A theist is someone who believes in God, but God in a more personal sense than the non-personal pantheist gods. In this view, God created the universe out of nothing and is a separate and distinct entity from the universe and the creation. The God of theism is eternal, immaterial, atemporal, non-spatial, and uncaused. Most theists believe that one can know God and have a relationship with Him. The major theistic religions of the world are Christianity, Judaism and Islam. These three religions represent about 55% of the world's population.

Why do you need to know about worldviews? Because they are all represented by the people we meet every day in one form or another. Many times they are merged together into a patchwork of religion by those who believe that all paths lead to God. Others believe they are all false. With many, Jesus is just one more religion in this confusing mix. This is why many young Christians, after leaving college, are confused about their faith. After growing up in a cocoon of Christianity, many students are unprepared when faced with this barrage of religious ideas. If you are a parent, this should concern you.

The purpose of this chapter is to help you engage other religious worldviews with good information, not to keep you from being exposed to them. As a Christian, you should embrace rational debate and open mindedness. You should also know when you've met a hyper-skeptic. A hyper-skeptic will never read anything from Christian scholars. They believe that Christian apologists are always lying and think the evidence for the flying spaghetti monster is as good as the evidence for God. They will not even agree with a Christian on topics that are undisputed in scholarly literature, and think that if they agree with a Christian they are aiding the destruction of civilization. Know who these people are and avoid having discussions on their terms.

The truth is, Christianity can be placed beside the other religions of the world and compared without fear of the influence of hyper-skeptics. Most people do not reject Christianity because they weighed it against some other worldview and found it wanting; they reject it because they did not weigh it at all. They saw something they liked in another religion, or atheism, and followed it. There was no careful weighing of the facts. The purpose of Christian apologetics is to keep people from doing that.

Do all paths lead to God?

In our modern world of rapid information exchange and blending of cultures, we are exposed to many different and conflicting ideas. The major religions of the world have long since made their presence known, but in the digital age, even obscure religious views are projected to a worldwide audience. Nowhere is this more obvious than YouTube and other websites where many are getting their information about religion.

How do Christians respond to this diversity of

religion? Some have embraced religious pluralism, which means that we should treat all religions the same because we are all on the same path to God. Other Christians try a more inclusive approach, believing that all people of different religions are saved by Christ, whether they know it or not.

Unfortunately, those who embrace pluralism must overlook some major contradictions. The first problem is that the religions of the world teach different things. At their core, all religions teach the opposite of what the pluralists claim, which is, that they alone have the truth about God.

For example, Islam makes the claim that other religions are false, which means that if Islam is true, as religious pluralism demands, then all other religions are false, which is impossible since all other religions are true. You see the problem? Everyone cannot be right, no matter how much we want them to be.

So when someone claims that all paths lead to God because all religions are basically the same, we should ask for some clarification, such as, what is a path? Major religions? Minor religions? What about the bazaar religions, like the church of marijuana? Does that path also lead to God? Who gets to decide the cutoff point for a valid religion?

You see, this is an impossible position to defend. Those who claim that all paths lead to God offer us no reason to accept this position. On the other hand, Jesus claimed to be the only path to salvation, and he provided evidence for his claims. As I've pointed out, Christianity can be tested against other religions of the world. How? Because only Christianity offers evidence from history, archaeology, science and philosophy to back up the exclusive claims of Jesus.

Is Christianity intolerant?

This is a popular notion in modern society. There is no doubt that you will hear someone say that Christians are intolerant because they try to tell other people how to live, how to believe, and worst of all, that Jesus is the only path to God.

Of course the problem is in our new politically correct definition of tolerance – which is to accept that all views have equal merit and no single view should be considered better or more reliable than any other.

In Merriam-Webster's original 1828 dictionary the word intolerant is defined as:

1. Not enduring; not able to endure. The powers of the human body being limited and intolerant of excesses.
2. Not enduring difference of opinion or worship; refusing to tolerate others in the enjoyment of their opinions, rights and worship.

This definition makes perfect sense in that it defines intolerance as the inability to endure a difference of opinion, or outright refusing to tolerate the opinions of others. This definition explicitly implies that tolerating others means that we do not interfere with their rights or religious practices. In other words, we do not go to war with them because of their opinions. However, it does not implicitly or explicitly imply that the opinions of others are accepted as equal to our own, but only that they are tolerated peacefully and without interference.

In the 2012 edition of the Webster's dictionary, the definition of intolerance is modified and reads as follows:

1. Unable or unwilling to endure.
2. Unwilling to grant equal freedom of expression especially in religious matters.
3. Unwilling to grant or share social, political, or professional rights: bigoted.

There is no outcry from the Christian community today to deny political or professional rights to anyone who holds a different viewpoint in America. But notice item 3 where the phrase 'social, political, or professional rights' has been added. This implies that if all social, political, or professional rights are not granted by the majority, then intolerance is assumed. Even so, you may ask how these rights are being denied. This addition to the definition of intolerance is primarily driven by those who seek same-sex marriage and view anyone who votes against it as intolerant. The definition also implicitly implies that to deny any of these rights is bigoted. The implication is that the majority is bigoted when exercising their constitutional right to vote against certain social issues, such as abortion, the legalization of drugs, and same-sex marriage.

This new definition represents a corruption of the English language. Tolerance has changed in meaning from tolerate, to agree. Now to simply disagree with someone verbally is to be intolerant. This new definition of tolerance may seem like a kind and benevolent position, but it is itself intolerant and leads to the suppression of honest debate. After all, no one wants to be called intolerant or bigoted just for claiming to be right about something. Furthermore, how can we have real debate when everyone is right? What would be the point?

The truth is, Christianity, or any other religion in the world, cannot accept everything in every other religion as true and still maintain its own belief system. Sure, most of the major religions in the world agree on many things, but how is that more important than where they disagree? These disagreements focus on some very important points: like the nature of God, the nature of mankind, the consequences of sin, the existence of evil, and what happens after we die. They cannot all be right while disagreeing on these fundamental issues. Different religions do not teach the same things, and as a result, they can't all be true.

Therefore, anyone who claims to be tolerant by this new definition is embracing contradiction. After all, even the most tolerant person in the world must at least be intolerant of intolerance, right?

This may seem like an extreme example, but it makes the point that I want to make, which is, that when anyone gives their opinion on anything they are by default disagreeing with the opposite view;

otherwise, they are living in contradiction with their own words.

Still, the mere fact that Christianity claims to be true is a big problem for many people today. Religion in America is becoming more pluralistic, meaning we must all accept each other's religion as true or be guilty of intolerance.

But consider this: We cannot simply believe everything is true and still live as rational human beings. Real tolerance is respect for other ideas, not a rejection of the concept of truth.

Why Not All Paths?

There are many who claim belief in God, but do not think we can know God, or think that all gods are the same. Others choose eastern religion, atheism, agnosticism, or some other 'ism.' The point is, the problems in these other worldviews can be exposed by comparing them to Christianity. In fact, Christianity should be compared to other worldviews to judge which view holds a more reasonable explanation of what we experience in reality. We can approach this in the same way we approach any other research project.

To seek the answer to a question is the most common form of research. We start with a hypothesis, which is an educated guess or question about the truth of some aspect of reality, and we work from there to establish a workable theory. After the hypothesis is formed, evidence is collected, data is analyzed, and conclusions are made based on the evidence. Rarely can any research results claim proof of a hypothesis. Research results typically support, or do not support, the hypothesis.

The way to apply this methodology to the truth claims of Christianity is to compare how Christianity stands up to the rigor of the research process compared to other religious worldviews. We can do this many ways, but here we will simply ask "Does Christianity agree with actual human experience and reality better than other worldviews?" In other words, does Christian theology agree with what we encounter in nature, science, history and personal human experience? Obviously, I think it does, but we can test this hypothesis by applying the same test we would to any hypothesis.

A good hypothesis needs to have several things in order to be viable. These are:

Falsifiable – Can be proven false.
Parsimony – The hypothesis with the fewest assumptions should be selected.
Explanatory strength – Explains reality as we see it.
Logical consistency – Non-contradicting.
Functional livability – Can be put into practice.

Think about this: A lot of people outside of core Christianity are claiming a lot of things about religion. But how much of what they say can be proven wrong? Nothing. That's why they hold such views. They intentionally take positions that cannot be falsified.

Remember, any statement that cannot be proven false is not a good hypothesis. For example, Mohammad claimed to have received the Quran word for word from the angel Gabriel. This is a core belief of Islam. You cannot prove this true or false. There were no witnesses and there is no historical evidence that can support it as true or false.

The followers of Hinduism and Buddhism base a majority of their teachings on reincarnation. However, since this happens after death, and no one can come back and report on it, it cannot be proved false? Atheists and naturalists hold as their core claim that life evolved from non-life; but how can we prove it did not happen when there were no witnesses and no one can go back in time and see it happen?

Of course, there are many aspects outside the core beliefs of these religious worldviews that can be easily falsified. For example, the Quran states that Jesus did not die on the cross; yet virtually every biblical historian (conservative, liberal and atheist) agree that Jesus was crucified by the Romans in the first century. There is ample first-century literature outside of the Bible to support this fact.

The Hindu scriptures (The Vedas) claim that the moon is 800,000 miles further away from the Earth than the sun; that the moon shines by its own light; that night is caused by the sun setting behind a large mountain; that the world is flat and triangular; and that the world is made of honey, sugar, butter and wine. All of which are easily falsifiable.

Now consider Christianity, which rests on the

resurrection of Jesus. All someone needs to do is prove the resurrection never happened and Christianity is defeated. Many have tried to do this, and still try, but the resurrection cannot be explained away through natural means. What this means is that, unlike any other religious worldview, Christianity's core belief can be falsified.

Parsimony, in this case meaning the simplest explanation is probably the most accurate, should be part of a good hypothesis. A problem with many different complex answers becomes quickly unsolvable. For example, some eastern religions, such as Hinduism, have hundreds of millions of gods. These pantheistic religions also believe in reincarnation, which represents a constant rebirth into the next life with no way of knowing how one may be reincarnated or how long the process will actually take.

Islam's message of submission to God is a non-complex message, but the complexity is in never knowing if your sin is greater than your good deeds. There is always a gray area for the Muslim, in that he must work his way into heaven by doing more good works than bad. Muslims who have converted to Christianity report that it is very hard to know where you stand with God at any given point, unless you are martyred.

The atheist version of where we come from is getting more non-parsimonious by the minute. Sixty years ago, scientists believed the universe was eternal. Now that we know the universe had a beginning, atheist scientists, looking for an explanation that does not involve God, have come up with the multiple universe theory. This theory is not falsifiable, and it is far from parsimonious. On the other hand, Christianity offers a message of salvation that a child can understand.

Islam is a monotheistic religion that points to a creator God that agrees with the Christian concept of God, and therefore has good explanatory strength where God is concerned. However, Islam fails to explain how one can effectively deal with the problem of sin.

The pantheist religions do not attempt to explain very many things. Hindus, Buddhists, Shintos and others in the east pride themselves on embracing contradiction, and it's hard to explain anything while embracing contradiction. Also, these religions claim that sin, evil and life itself are all an illusion. This does very little to explain the reality we experience. In fact, it is a way to avoid explaining anything.

Of course, the atheists can offer no explanation for the fundamental questions that people ask: Who are we, where do we come from, what is our purpose, what happens after we die. However, Christianity explains the nature of God, the nature of man, sin, the problem of evil, and what happens in the afterlife.

Christianity offers logical consistency by describing reality in a way consistent with what we experience as human beings. In other words, it fits existing recognized knowledge. For example, if God exists, then the claims of Jesus are reasonable because supernatural events are possible. There is no problem here in logic.

The Christian worldview does not claim that the world is an illusion, or that deliberate contradictions in logic are acceptable like eastern religions often claim.

The Atheist worldview also fails the test of logical consistency on many levels. It is logically incoherent, philosophically bankrupt, and historically unsound. For example, atheism is so logically inconsistent with its view of morality that it cannot be taken literally, for to do so would lead one to a level of moral repugnance unthinkable even to an atheist. This can easily be illustrated by suggesting to atheists that babies born with birth defects should be killed. Even though this blatant immoral act would be rejected by most atheists, they have no moral ground to stand on other than that provided by theists. Atheists believe there is no God and therefore no objective moral standard upon which to base right and wrong. Yet they demand the moral law of Christianity without moral obligation to God. This is a staggering logical inconsistency.

Finally, functional livability is possible with Christianity in a way not possible with other religious worldviews. It seems that the only other livable worldview would be complete indifference to God or any of the big questions of life. Some people seem to live that way, but it's not likely they really do.

Atheism is not livable for most people because of objective moral values and duties. Remember, the atheist claims to accept that God does not exist and therefore objective moral duties also do not exist, but they rarely live that way. This holds true for the eastern religions when they teach that all of reality is an illusion. But do they really live that way? Does the person who claims that life is an illusion look both ways before crossing the street? Of course, because no one can actually live as if life is illusory. Many who practice pantheism also claim that contradiction is OK, but to make that claim they must assert that the opposite claim – that contradiction leads to serious problems - is wrong; which is a contradiction and should not matter anyway. That may be confusing, but the point is, to deny that the basic laws of logic exist, you must use the basic laws of logic to make the denial in the first place. It is an incoherent and unlivable position.

Christianity is livable because there is a solution for sin, an explanation for the existence of the universe and ourselves, and a path to God that is not dependent on us being good enough – which any honest person knows is impossible.

Conclusion

In light of modern historical data, Christianity offers significant evidence that is rational and historically grounded. If you compare this to any other religion in the world, you will see that no such evidence is offered. You are simply told to believe with nothing more than their word and your personal feelings.

Worse, what you hear today is a confusing hodgepodge of spirituality that is admittedly made-up to satisfy the individual's personal beliefs. It's hard to say which is worse: being duped by a false religion, or being duped by your own self-delusion.

Please understand that none of this proves that Christianity is true with mathematical certainty, it just makes Christianity a more reasonable explanation that best explains a broad range of human experiences; which, of course, means that it's true.

The problem is that Jesus is not as popular today as He was when I was a young. In fact, there is a considerable amount of hostility toward Christianity in the public square. This is due to a distorted view of Christians and Jesus. As Christians, we are ambassadors of Christ and our job is to help others know the real Jesus; and in order to do that, we must know the real Jesus.

CHAPTER FIVE

The Resurrection

"If Jesus rose from the dead, then you have to accept all that he said; if he didn't rise from the dead, then why worry about any of what he said? The issue on which everything hangs is not whether or not you like his teaching but whether or not he rose from the dead."

— Timothy Keller

From the very beginning, skeptics have tried to prove that Christ did not rise from the dead. After all, if the resurrection can be shown false, then Christians are defeated. Nonetheless, it turns out that it is not so easy to dismiss the resurrection as fantasy. If fact, it is getting harder every day to claim the resurrection is false based on the current evidence. What surprises many people is that much of this evidence comes from sources outside the Bible. This does not mean we cannot use the New Testament to support the resurrection. Many well-known Christian apologists, such as Josh McDowell, do that very well. It is a legitimate argument to make considering how great an ancient source we have in the New Testament documents. Even skeptics point to parts of the New Testament and cite them as reliable historical texts. This does not mean the resurrection of Christ is accepted as fact, but the documents are accepted as legitimate eyewitness accounts from the time of Christ.

One of the most attested New Testament texts is 1 Corinthians. In chapter fifteen, Paul quotes an early church creed that predates the writing of his epistle to the church in Corinth.

"For I delivered to you as of first importance what I also received: that Christ died for our sins in accordance with the Scriptures, that he was buried, that he was raised on the third day in accordance with the Scriptures, and that he appeared to Cephas, then to the twelve. Then he appeared to more than five hundred brothers at one time, most of whom are still alive, though some have fallen asleep. Then he appeared to James, then to all the apostles. Last of all, as to one untimely born, he appeared also to me."

-1 Corinthians 15: 3-8

Because this text is accepted as authentic by liberal, conservative, and atheist Bible scholars, it serves to demonstrate the legitimacy of the New Testament as a historical source. The significance of this creed is that it predates the writing of 1 Corinthians, which is dated by the most liberal scholars at around 54 AD. Why does that matter? Paul was converted to the faith around 34 AD, and three years later first met with the apostles in Jerusalem. It was then that he received this creed. This dates the existence of this record to only seven years after the resurrection of Christ. The writing is too close to the actual events to be myth or legend. In other words, there was not enough time for the information to be skewed by time, or corrupted by translation. Therefore, the 1 Corinthians 15 creed is accepted by skeptics as extremely close to the actual events in history. Very few documents from antiquity that record historical events are this well attested.

Clearly the New Testament makes a powerful case for the resurrection. However, if we briefly turn our attention from the highly accurate records in the New Testament and focus on modern scholarship, we find a growing body of evidence that also supports the resurrection. This evidence comes from a diverse group of New Testament scholars, many of which are skeptics.

Gary Habermas reviewed the literature on the resurrection from 2400 English, German and French sources from 1975 to present (Habermas, 2004). These sources are taken from the entire spectrum of liberal to conservative scholars, many of which are atheists. After analysis of the data, Habermas identified twelve minimum facts about the resurrection agreed upon by an overwhelming majority of scholars (at least 90%). These facts are:

1. Jesus died by crucifixion.
2. He was buried.
3. His death caused the disciples to despair and lose hope, believing His life had ended.
4. The grave (tomb) was empty a few days later.
5. The disciples had experiences which they believed were literal appearances of the risen Jesus.
6. The disciples were transformed from doubters to bold witnesses.
7. The resurrection was the central message in early church preaching.
8. They preached the message of Jesus' resurrection in Jerusalem first.
9. As a result of this preaching, the Church was born and grew.
10. Sunday became the primary day of worship.
11. James was converted to the faith after he believed he saw the risen Christ.
12. Paul was converted to the faith after he believed he saw the risen Christ.

These are potent facts we can use to test theories concerning the resurrection. After all, if these twelve statements are facts that even atheist critics accept, then the truth about the resurrection must fit all of these facts. Any theory about the resurrection will fit some of these facts, no matter how radical the notion. However, if all twelve do not fit, then the theory must be discarded.

Beginning in the first century, accusations and

assumptions about events on the first Easter Sunday had already spread throughout the Roman Empire. Since then, skeptics have attempted to use naturalist theories to explain why the tomb was empty, or why the apostles believed Jesus rose from the dead. With the twelve minimal facts, we can test these theories and determine if they fit the known facts. Also, to a lesser extent, I will apply the same criteria used by historians to determine the best explanation of ancient events: explanatory scope, explanatory power, probability, alignment with accepted beliefs, level of ad hoc material, and ability to surpass rival theories. The twelve minimal facts coupled with common historical criteria are powerful methods to answer skeptics, or help those who want to believe but struggle with the concept of a bodily resurrection of Jesus.

The Apostles Stole the Body

This is the oldest explanation for the missing body of Jesus. It is mentioned in Matthew 28 and also refuted. This explanation of the resurrection places blame on the disciples and accuses them of stealing the body.

> *While they were going, behold, some of the guard went into the city and told the chief priests all that had taken place. And when they had assembled with the elders and taken counsel, they gave a sufficient sum of money to the soldiers and said, "Tell people, 'His disciples came by night and stole him away*

while we were asleep.' And if this comes to the governor's ears, we will satisfy him and keep you out of trouble." So they took the money and did as they were directed. And this story has been spread among the Jews to this day.

-Matthew 28:11-15 (ESV)

When the gospel of Matthew was written, this rumor was still being spread in Jerusalem. Since the book of Matthew was written around 50 AD, this story was already 20 years old. Polycarp, a student of John, wrote about this accusation in 110 AD as well as Tertullian in 130 AD. Furthermore, Justin Martyr writing in 150 AD, also attested to this accusation by the Jewish authorities and reported that it was still being spread 120 years later. Many others have perpetuated the story over the years, although few scholars support it today.

Although this accusation against the disciples explains facts 1, 2 and the empty tomb, it fails to explain any of the other known facts about the resurrection. Remember, there are twelve well established facts that need to be explained before we have a viable natural explanation for the resurrection of Jesus and the actions of the apostles that followed. Therefore, this theory fails on facts three, and five through twelve. Any of these facts could be explored to make the point, but fact #6 is all that is needed to defeat a stolen body theory.

The apostles became bold proclaimers of the faith because they experienced the risen Lord. St. Augustine

(354AD – 430AD) described them as 'simple and lowly men' who changed the world. How could such men boldly proclaim the risen Christ in the face of persecution from the Jewish leaders and the Roman authorities if they did not believe their own message? They knew the result of their faith was persecution. The religious leaders had just crucified Jesus; so how could the apostles think they would not suffer the same fate? Would they so willingly die for a lie?

Many argue that religious zealots have died for false beliefs throughout history. In fact, it is nothing new. But unlike terrorists who fly planes into buildings or strap bombs on their chests, the apostles knew the truth. If they stole the body, then they knew that Christ did not rise. However, their actions contradict that fact. Unlike liars acting selfishly for money or power, the apostles defied the authorities and proclaimed the risen Lord. In doing so they refused to obey the religious leaders in Jerusalem, and refused to call Caesar Lord. These actions only served to bring persecution and death – not power or money. Common sense tells us that the apostles had nothing to gain and everything to lose by making up this lie. As a result, we can be certain that the apostles did not steal the body of Jesus and claim He was raised.

The Wrong Tomb Theory

This theory falls into a category of theories that claim the body of Jesus was lost. The wrong tomb theory was made popular by Kirsopp Lake (1872–1946) of Harvard Divinity School. Lake argued that the woman went to the wrong tomb because there were so many similar tombs around Jerusalem. They found an open tomb and a young man who told them "Jesus is not here." The frightened women mistook the young man for an angel and fled. As a result, the rumor of the resurrection began and Christianity was born.

The wrong tomb theory answers facts number one, two, three and four, but nothing else. It does not explain the experience of the apostles, James or Paul. It does not explain the zeal of the early church and the growth that followed. It does not explain why the apostles thought they saw the risen Lord. Therefore, a missing body is not enough to transform the apostles from doubters to bold proclaimers.

A similar theory is the missing body hypothesis promoted by John Dominic Crossan of the Jesus seminar. Crossan argues that Jesus was taken down from the cross and thrown in a shallow mass grave and later eaten by dogs. Since the disciples could not find His body, they assumed a resurrection. Again, this explanation only fits three of the twelve facts. The main fact that it claims to fit – the missing body – does not fit very well when examining the evidence. First, not all crucifixion victims were buried in mass graves as Crossan claims (Craig, 1994). More importantly, the Bible names Joseph of Arimathea as a member of the high council who donated his tomb to Jesus. If the apostles made up this story and circulated it among Jerusalem in the first century (see fact #8), it could have easily been falsified, since a wealthy member of the

Sanhedrin would be known by many. Moreover, if the women and the apostles went to the wrong tomb and proclaimed the resurrection, the Sanhedrin could have simply asked Joseph of Arimathea to show them the actual tomb so they could expose the resurrection as false.

The wrong tomb theory fails miserably when considering explanatory scope. It does not account for the events that followed Jesus' death. The incredible growth and proliferation of Christianity is unprecedented in history. Christianity started as a humble and peaceful movement that quickly gained converts from former enemies. Moreover, within 250 years the disciples of Jesus overwhelmed the Roman Empire without drawing a sword.

When considering the impact left on history by the death of Jesus and the events that followed, it's clear that something big happened. A missing body can be explained many ways. Only a weak hypothesis would assume that so many different people would believe that Jesus rose from the dead just because the body could not be found. We have no reason to believe that first century Jews would so readily accept a resurrection from the dead with no evidence. A missing body is not significant enough to trigger the events that birthed Christianity. This is like believing something insignificant caused the big meteor crater in Arizona. This impressive impact crater is one mile wide and 550 feet deep. Obviously, something big and powerful was the cause. To claim that Christianity began on nothing more than the news of a missing body is like arguing that the crater was caused by a BB gun. Christianity left a massive crater in history, and that crater must have been cause by something big. A missing body is not enough to leave behind a historical impact that size.

According to William Lane Craig, there are no conflicting traditions to the empty tomb story anywhere in the ancient literature, even in the Jewish polemic (Craig, 1994). There is no doubt that the tomb of Jesus was in a well-known location, owned by a well-known person, and empty. The resurrection message could not have been preached in Jerusalem and accepted by so many if the empty tomb was not established as a fact.

The Apostles Hallucinated

Another proposed theory claims that the Apostles Hallucinated. Revived in modern times by Gerd Ludemann, this hypothesis argues that the apostles were so overcome with guilt and emotion at the loss of Jesus that their minds projected hallucinations of the risen Lord (Ludemann, 2004). According to Ludemann, this was particularly the case with Peter and Paul, who became the primary proponents of the risen Christ by becoming as hallucinatory enablers for the other disciples.

The hallucination hypothesis does not fit all the facts and therefore falls woefully short of explaining the resurrection of Jesus. At best, it can explain why a couple of the apostles believed they saw Jesus alive after the crucifixion, but it fails on almost every other point. First, the body would also have to be missing and its location unknown to the Jewish or Roman authorities. If the apostles were hallucinating, then who stole the body? A missing body along with hallucinations is even more unlikely than just a missing body (probability theory) and lacks explanatory strength on most of the known facts.

The hallucination hypothesis is also highly improbable based on 150 years of psychiatric research on hallucinations. According to the American Psychological Association, mass hallucinations are extremely rare, if they exist at all (Copan and Tacelli, 2000). The APA argues that visual hallucinations themselves are rare, occurring in only about 7% of the cases and primarily to the elderly when grieving the loss of a loved one. This does not fit well with the fact that all the apostles believed they saw Jesus raised from the dead (fact #5), as well as James and Paul (facts 11 & 12). Even if an extreme state of mind caused these mass hallucinations, as proposed by Ludemann, not all of these people were in the same state of mind. For example, Jesus appeared to friends and foes alike. James, the brother of Jesus, was not a follower and did not accept Him as the Messiah. However, after the death of Jesus, James had an experience that transformed him into a disciple and a leader in the Church. As recorded by the Jewish historian Josephus, James was martyred for his faith in Christ. What would it take for someone to accept their own brother as God incarnate and die for that belief? Logical consistency tells us that it would take something extraordinary. Therefore, hallucinations alone do not explain James' conversion to Christianity.

Paul's conversion to the faith is even harder to explain by hallucinations. Paul was not only skeptical; he was out to persecute, imprison, and kill Christians. Paul was not in a grieving or guilt-ridden state of mind. None of the seven epistles that critics agree were written by Paul offer any evidence that Paul was feeling guilty for persecuting Christians. On the contrary, Paul declares his former intentions on several occasions in his epistles. He never alluded to any desire to join the Christian movement or sympathize with Jesus. Therefore, no evidence exists in the early church documents that Paul had any propensity to turn to Christianity on his own. To argue, as Ludemann does, that Paul had a personal struggle with his Jewish faith and an attraction to Christianity is totally ad hoc. There is not a speck of evidence to support this claim. Considering what historians and scholars actually know about Paul, his conversion is impossible to explain without a miraculous event.

Some have argued that the disciples were experiencing delusions, not hallucinations. Small groups of people do sometimes share dangerously false beliefs (Kyriacou, 2011). One example was the Church of Venus headed by Marshall Applewhite. This group was convinced that a spaceship was coming to rescue them from Earth. As a result, they committed mass suicide. The followers of Jim Jones suffered the same fate. The problem with applying this theory to the resurrection is multifaceted. First, we still have an empty tomb. Second, Paul was not of the same mindset as the apostles and was not a candidate for their shared delusion. Third, the same can be said for James, who was a skeptic before the resurrection.

Hallucinations or delusions brought on by grief or guilt can only explain a few of the twelve known facts about the resurrection. The theory simply does not fit the historical data and is weak when explaining the events surrounding the resurrection.

The Swoon Theory

An old theory that has lost much of its credibility today is the Swoon Theory. This theory was first offered by Karl Friedrich Bahrdt (1741-1792) in the 18th century. The hypothesis states that Jesus did not die on the cross, but merely passed out. After being taken down from the cross and placed in the tomb, Jesus woke up and presented himself to the apostles.

In their 1982 book Holy Blood, Holy Grail, Michael Baigent, Richard Leigh and Henry Lincoln also argue that Jesus did not die on the cross, but that he was given a toxin that made him appear dead. After being taken off the cross, Jesus was revived. As a result, He was able to appear to his disciples before escaping to France with Mary Magdalene. Dan Brown based his blockbuster novel, The Di Vinci Code, on this premise.

This theory seems to fit the known facts very well on first inspection, except fact #1 – Jesus died! It would also be a very strong theory if it were not impossible.

The reason this theory fails with the majority of Bible scholars and historians today is because we know so much more about crucifixion. As a result of this knowledge, we can reject the idea that anyone could survive a Roman crucifixion. This is why fact #1 is on the list of known facts.

In Bahrdt's day, there was certainty among skeptical Bible scholars that Jesus was crucified. However, it's possible that someone could appear dead and wake up at some point later. Jesus may have been in a coma for a few hours, and then snapped out of it in the tomb. This is known to happen in modern times (without the tomb) so why not the first century?

The answer to the swoon theory, or any apparent death theory, is that crucifixion was 100% lethal. In fact, historians and physicians who have studied crucifixion argue that it is no more survivable than jumping off the Empire State Building. In 1986, Edwards, Gabel & Hosmer published an article in the well-respected Journal of the American Medical Association on the impossibility of Jesus surviving the resurrection.

Jesus of Nazareth underwent Jewish and Roman trials, was flogged, and was sentenced to death by crucifixion. The scourging produced deep stripelike lacerations and appreciable blood loss, and it probably set the stage for hypovolemic shock, as evidenced by the fact that Jesus was too weakened to carry the crossbar (patibulum) to Golgotha. At the site of crucifixion, his wrists were nailed to the patibulum and, after the patibulum was lifted onto the upright post (stipes), his feet were nailed to the stipes. The major pathophysiologic effect of crucifixion was an interference with normal respirations. Accordingly, death resulted primarily from hypovolemic shock and exhaustion asphyxia. Jesus' death was ensured by the thrust of a soldier's spear into his side. Modern medical interpretation of the historical evidence indicates that Jesus was dead when taken down from the cross (p. 1459).

The Romans combined scourging with crucifixion to ensure the victim was already in a near death state before being hung on the cross. Nevertheless, the main cause of death during crucifixion was asphyxiation. While hanging on a cross with no support under the feet, the victim could not breathe properly and suffocated as a result.

The Jewish historian Josephus witnessed five Roman crucifixions during the first century and reported that victims were dying so quickly that the Romans changed the method to extend the suffering (Whiston, 2009).

"I saw many captives crucified, and remembered three of them as my former acquaintance. I was very sorry at this in my mind, and went with tears in my eyes to Titus, and told him of them; so he immediately commanded them to be taken down, and to have the greatest care taken of them, in order to their recovery; yet two of them died under the physician's hands, while the third recovered."

A method employed by the Romans to keep the victims alive longer was to place a block under the feet, or nail the feet, so the victim could push themselves up and breathe. This inflicted extreme pain on the victim as he pushed against the nail wounds, tearing the flesh in order to gasp for air. On occasions when the executioners wanted to offer mercy to the victim, they simply broke the legs (as reported in the Gospels). This prevented the victim from pushing up to breathe. Death by asphyxiation followed quickly.

The skeptical German scholar D.F. Strauss (1808-1874) destroyed the swoon theory by arguing that it was totally implausible for Jesus to survive scourging and crucifixion, unwrap Himself from the burial cloth, push away the heavy stone, walk to the apostles on pierced and torn feet, and present Himself as the victoriously risen Lord. If Jesus appeared to the apostles in this condition, His defeat of death and the cross would not be very convincing. The only thing the apostles would be convinced of is that their Lord needed immediate medical attention.

Even if the aforementioned scenario were possible, it would not cause the apostles to believe that Jesus defeated death, but only that He was very lucky to be alive. Facts five and six make it clear that the apostles were changed men because they believed they saw Jesus raised from the dead, not in a near-death state. It defies logic to accept a hypothesis that relies so heavily on this flawed premise of surviving a Roman crucifixion and presenting oneself as raised from the dead in a glorious body (Philippians 3:21).

The Myth/Legend Theory

The myth/legend theory is the predominate hypothesis among academics. However, these academics are rarely Bible scholars or historians who study ancient documents. According to this theory, Jesus was a religious leader who amassed a large following. After angering the Jewish and Roman authorities, He was crucified and buried. In most cases the hypothesis states that His followers never claimed He rose from the dead; yet stories were told over the years that became embellished with supernatural myths and claims of His deity. These legends were written into the Bible; and as a result, the myths spread and the Church grew.

This explanation resonates with people today. After all, we can all relate to rumors and urban legends that are told and retold until they scarcely resemble the original truth. Add two thousand years of telling and retelling, and it's hard to believe the truth remains. People can't even convey accurate information in a simple news story today, so how can a story told 2000 years ago be accurate?

Even so, the myth/legend theory does not explain the resurrection of Jesus, the actions of the apostles, and the growth of Christianity for many reasons. First, when we consider the agreed upon twelve facts it becomes obvious that the myth/legend theory fits none of them. To only name a few, it does not explain the empty tomb, the apostle's belief that Jesus rose from the dead, and the conversion of the persecutor Paul only three years later. If the resurrection and the foundation of Christianity is all a myth, then we should have strong evidence that nothing significant happened in the first century surrounding the life of Christ. The evidence would show that many years later the stories appeared on the scene and began to influence people and history. But this is not what we learn from the historical evidence. The accounts of the resurrection found in the New Testament are very early eyewitness reports written by the eyewitnesses themselves, or those who had direct contact with eyewitnesses.

To consider what a myth looks like, we need only consider the teachings of Buddha. The earliest writing of Buddha's teaching appeared 400 years after his death (Schumann, 2003). During that time, oral tradition was the only record of his teachings. Although oral tradition was a legitimate method for preserving historical information, 400 years is plenty of time for embellishments to seep in and distort the truth. With no early documents to reference, the followers of Buddha were dependent on word of mouth to preserve the traditions for centuries.

Conversely, the early Christian oral traditions were written down and preserved within a few years of the resurrection. 1 Corinthians 15:3-8 holds an example of an early church creed, or oral tradition, which was recorded by Paul only 25 years after the resurrection. Based on early manuscripts of the New Testament, we know this creed is accurately preserved. Furthermore, critical scholars believe that the book of 1 Corinthians was written by Paul and dates to 55 AD. According to Paul, he received this creed much earlier than he wrote 1 Corinthians.

If the story of Jesus rising from the dead was a mythical event added later by overzealous followers, then early verifiable accounts would show no evidence of a resurrection. But the claims of a resurrection are present from the beginning, and therefore must be explained by natural means if one takes a skeptical approach. Nonetheless, no natural theory fits the known facts.

The bottom line is that myths need time to grow. In other words, they require an environment in which to incubate where the legends cannot be challenged by the facts. We know the apostles preached the resurrection in Jerusalem immediately after the death of Jesus (fact #6). Anyone could have exposed these claims if they were false, but no one did. All we have in the ancient literature outside the New Testament are theories explaining what happened, not outright denials that Jesus was who He claimed to be.

The Twin Theory

A more recent theory to enter the scholarly debate is the twin theory offered by Greg Cavin (2009). This theory claims that Jesus had a twin brother who lived in another area of Israel. Shortly after Jesus died, the twin brother arrived in Jerusalem and was worshiped as the risen Christ. This hypothesis is better than most and fits all of the facts except two very important ones: #4 and #11.

A major weakness of this theory is the empty tomb. Even if a twin of Jesus showed up and stepped into the role of risen Lord, that would not remove all doubts from skeptics – even the apostles. Peter and John ran to the tomb to see for themselves upon news of the risen Jesus. If a twin of Jesus appeared on the scene, it would only require one curious doubter to take a short walk and check the tomb. Since there were so many doubters, even some among the apostles, this simple test could easily expose the twin as an imposter.

Fact #11 is also problematic. James, the brother of Jesus, was converted to the faith after believing he saw the risen Jesus. The problem here is that James would have known his own brother, even if the twin was unknown to him from birth. On the other hand, if James knew he had a brother who was Jesus' twin, then only a conspiracy would explain the twin being proclaimed as the risen Jesus. If the apostles, or only James, knew that the resurrection was a fraud, then this theory has many of the same problems as the stolen body theory. For the twin theory to have any chance of being taken seriously, the twin must have fooled the apostles. But this seems impossible based on the events from history and superior rival theories.

To seriously consider a twin taking the place of Jesus and fooling his disciples, we must make several grandiose assumptions. First, if twin Jesus lives in another village, he would certainly have a different accent or dialect. In a time without rapid communication and transportation, coming from over the hill was like coming from another country (Hazen,

2009). We have to assume no one would notice this and get suspicious. Second, other mannerisms and personality traits would be different in twin Jesus and easily recognized by his closest followers, especially his own brother. It's totally unrealistic to assume that no one would notice that twin Jesus was a different person. After all, people do not rise from the dead every day. There would be many questions, and as a result, this claim would quickly fall apart.

The Substitution Theory

The substitution theory argues that Jesus did not die on the cross, but that someone else, perhaps a look-alike, died in his place. As a result, Jesus could claim to have risen from the dead before escaping to Europe and leave some hapless substitute to die on the cross and do the dirty work for the church. Obviously, this theory fails to fit the facts of history. Fact number one says that Jesus died! Without going any further we have a major conflict with the historical evidence.

First, if Jesus skipped out on the crucifixion and went to Europe, then how did he appear to Paul two years later? It is generally believed that Paul's encounter with Jesus happened about two to three years after the crucifixion. If so, did Jesus hop on a plane and jet back to meet Paul on the Damascus road, only to disappear again? Not likely. There is majority consensus among skeptical scholars that Paul thought he saw the risen Jesus. This is impossible to explain using the substitute theory.

Second, many extra-Biblical sources confirm that Jesus died by Roman crucifixion. There is no evidence in any of the ancient literature that a substitute died on the cross for Jesus. For example, Flavius Josephus (37-97 AD) wrote:

"Pilate condemned him to be crucified and to die. And those who had become his disciples did not abandon his discipleship. They reported that he had appeared to them three days after his crucifixion and that he was alive."

This account supports the Biblical record of Jesus' death on the cross and the reaction of the apostles. The Jewish Talmud, compiled between 70 and 200 AD, records that *"On the eve of the Passover Yeshu was hanged."* There is no suspicion in this hostile account that Jesus somehow evaded the death sentence. Furthermore, an anti-Christian Greek satirist named Lucian of Samosata (125AD-180AD) wrote:

"The Christians, you know, worship a man to this day--the distinguished personage who introduced their novel rites, and was crucified on that account" (as quoted by Fowler, 1905, p. 107).

The complete lack of evidence in the ancient literature that a substitute died for Jesus must be considered when analyzing this theory of the crucifixion. Like other naturalists theories of the resurrection, the substitute theory is flippant in its attempt to explain away the first century events with a hypothesis totally unsupported by the historical evidence or sound reason.

Possibly the biggest problem with the substitution theory is that it requires conspiracy. As previously stated, a conspiracy involving the apostles implies they were willing to suffer persecution, torture and death for something they knew was a lie. This is an incoherent understanding of human behavior. Maybe one mentally handicapped person would act in such a bizarre manner, but not all of Jesus' disciples - and certainly not James or Paul.

The Alien Theory

Theories to explain the resurrection of Jesus by natural means have no bounds. In fact, some are out of this world. The best of these theories (by 'best' I mean most amusing) is that Jesus was a space alien. Unlike other naturalistic theories of the resurrection, this theory does not come from a scholarly source, but from shrill voices on the internet that have the ability to reach millions with unsophisticated arguments.

The first thing to admit about this theory is that it actually explains all twelve historical facts. If Jesus was a space alien with advanced technology that dwarfs what we have today, then he could have performed some really neat tricks. For example, with a few Star Trek devices He could have beamed himself into rooms, walked through walls, healed the sick and tricked the Romans into believing he was dead on the cross. Moreover, being a powerful space alien explains how Jesus could have appeared to Paul in a blinding light and convinced James that his own brother, who to James was an embarrassment, had risen from the dead and was actually the awaited Messiah. More importantly, it explains everything that I've ever needed explained about anything. For example, why that cute girl dumped me in middle school – aliens got to her (or maybe she was a space alien and decided she did not like humans after all); why I did not turn in my homework in high school – aliens beamed it up to their ship just as I was reaching into my notebook; and I'm positive aliens are to blame for that time I crashed into a new Cadillac driven by an angry attorney.

Obviously I'm not treating this theory of the resurrection seriously. However, since many people consider this explanation possible, I will attempt to address it critically. But instead of laboring over the historical facts, this theory can be debunked by turning to simple philosophy.

In philosophy, an ad hoc explanation means that someone has added an irrelevant, off-the-point hypotheses to a theory in order to prevent it from being falsified. It is an explanation designed to fit the question, not an answer to the question as a result of research, historical data, or the scientific method. In other words, a hypothesis that explains everything, explains nothing. As I pointed out with slight sarcasm, you can explain anything with the alien theory – and that is what makes it worthless as an explanation.

An ad hoc explanation is not to be confused with

claiming that God acted on some historical event. The scientific method cannot be applied to God since He is a supernatural transcendent being that created nature and therefore is not part of nature. The scientific method can only talk to us about natural cause and effect, which makes it an ineffective tool for answering questions that only philosophy can hope to answer.

On the other hand, if space aliens exist they are part of nature, just like human beings and grasshoppers. It is the responsibility of science to prove that aliens exist or have visited the earth. But there is no such evidence. In fact, respectable scientists do not like to talk about little green men playing games on our minds and abducting people. Therefore, the alien theory can be summarily dismissed as ad hoc. If that troubles you, blame it on the aliens.

A Spiritual Resurrection

The final objection to the resurrection analyzed here is not really an objection at all. A common argument among believers is that Jesus rose in spirit, but not in physical form. The proponents of a spiritual resurrection believe that Jesus rose in spirit, presented Himself to the apostles and others, and then ascended into heaven. This belief stems from a liberal form of Christianity that seeks to interpret the Bible against a natural science background. Since people do not naturally rise from the dead, these skeptics argue that the resurrection must be spiritual only. Unfortunately, some professing Christians have difficulties accepting miracles and feel that a spiritual resurrection is less offensive to modern science.

According to Habermas and Licona (2004), liberal Bible scholars who do not accept the Gospels as actual writings of the apostles, do accept most of Paul's epistles as the legitimate writings of Paul. These scholars, who deny a bodily resurrection of Jesus, argue that Paul never confirms in plain language that Jesus rose physically. Moreover, skeptics point to Paul's encounter with Jesus on the Damascus road as evidence, since the appearance seems to be more spiritual than physical.

Now as he went on his way, he approached Damascus, and suddenly a light from heaven shone around him. And falling to the ground he heard a voice saying to him, "Saul, Saul, why are you persecuting me?" And he said, "Who are you, Lord?" And he said, "I am Jesus, whom you are persecuting.
-Acts 9:3-5

Others argue that the resurrection was existential and only occurred in the hearts of believers (Lüdemann , 2004). However, this is not a Christian view since it denies any form of actual resurrection – spiritual or physical. Still, others argue that it does not matter if the resurrection was physical or spiritual - Christ still rose. But this view ignores the overwhelming testimony in the New Testament and the writings of early church leaders that clearly asserts that Jesus rose in bodily form (Dunn, 1985).

The first problem with a spiritual only resurrection is the empty tomb. Had Jesus risen in spirit only, his body would have remained decaying in the grave. But this scenario is clearly refuted by a missing body, which is an agreed upon fact. Did the risen spiritual Jesus tell the apostles to go hide his body? This defies common sense. If Christ rose spiritually and convinced his disciples and others of this fact, then why would they care about the body in the tomb?

Furthermore, in 1 Corinthians 15:3-4 Paul recites the oral tradition that *"Christ died for our sins in accordance with the Scriptures, that he was buried, that he was raised on the third day in accordance with the Scriptures."* Here we have a creed that dates within a couple of years of the crucifixion. Paul received this creed from Peter and James five years after the resurrection, making this very early testimony that undeniably implies a bodily resurrection (Habermas, 1996).

Evidence that Paul's Damascus road experience did not convince him that Jesus rose spiritually can be found in Acts 13. Here, Paul is reported by Luke as saying that Jesus' body did not decay in the tomb like King David's. Also, in 1 Corinthians 15, Paul makes the analogy of a seed being planted and growing from the earth into a new body to describe the resurrection.

"It is sown a natural body; it is raised a spiritual body. There is a natural body, and there is a spiritual body"

-1 Cor. 15.44

Paul calls the raised body a body (soma) and not a spirit (pneuma). This explicitly implies a bodily resurrection, not a spiritual resurrection. Paul could have used an analogy to describe a spiritual resurrection of the body, but he did not. He certainly had the linguistics skills to use the exact Greek words to describe a spirit, but he did not.

The New Testament offers more compelling proof that Paul believed in a physical resurrection of Jesus. In Galatians 1:16-17 Paul explains how he decided not to immediately seek out the apostles after his encounter with Jesus:

> *"...I did not immediately consult with anyone; nor did I go up to Jerusalem to those who were apostles before me, but I went away into Arabia..."*

It was three years before Paul returned to Jerusalem. During that time, he spent fifteen days with Peter and James, the brother of Jesus. This was most likely the time when Paul received the 1 Corinthians 15 creed. Afterwards, Paul was away for fourteen years preaching the risen Jesus before returning to Jerusalem. Upon his return, he met with the apostles and "set before them" the Gospel he had preached to ensure that he had not "run in vain." Paul was comparing his version of the gospel to the Apostle's version. In Galatians 2:6, Paul declares that the apostles, "added nothing to me." The point is that Paul was not teaching a different Gospel than the apostles, who obviously believed that Jesus rose in bodily form.

There is no ambiguity about a bodily resurrection in the four gospels. If Paul was preaching a spiritual resurrection he would be at odds with Peter, John, and James who saw the risen Jesus, touched Him, and ate with Him. Virtually all scholars consider Paul a reliable source. Therefore, skeptics must take seriously Paul's report that his version of the Gospel and the resurrection was consistent with the original apostles. Although Paul's Damascus road experience seemed more spiritual than physical, Paul still preached a bodily resurrection. Furthermore, Paul's encounter with Jesus was years after the experiences of the apostles and Christ's ascension into heaven. This may explain why Jesus appeared to Paul in a unique way.

Based on the known facts, Paul's testimony, and the four Gospels, a spiritual resurrection fails to accurately describe the risen Christ. The eyewitnesses describe a physically risen Jesus and Paul never refutes that assertion. Moreover, the tomb was empty. Therefore, Christians who want to cling to a spiritual resurrection should consider the historical facts and the testimony in their own Bibles carefully.

Conclusion

One of the 20th century's most notable atheist philosophers and New Testament experts, Antony Flew (1923-2010), agreed with the twelve minimal facts of the resurrection. Before his death in 2010, Flew acknowledged his agreement and admitted he did not have an answer to the historical facts of the events in first century Jerusalem. His best explanation was that the apostles hallucinated, which turns out not to fit the very same facts he accepted as legitimate. However, according to the New York Times (2010) Flew, an outspoken atheist, stunned and dismayed his unbelieving followers when he announced in 2004 that God probably did exist. Unfortunately, this admission did not compel Flew to become a Christian, but the admission was significant for several reasons.

First, the facts of history are on the side of Christianity. To consider the evidence for the events of the first century and discount them as easily explainable is incoherent. The resurrection cannot be explained as foul play by the apostles, or a missing body, or hallucinations, or space aliens. This is the philosophical equivalent of trying to fit a square peg into a round hole – it just does not work.

Second, the scholarly community is finally starting to accept many of the facts that Christian apologists have argued for centuries. When a distinguished atheist like Flew accepts the facts and takes a baby step in the direction of God, it may not seem significant; however, Flew was not just any atheist. He influenced millions in his lifetime with his books and lectures on the authenticity of atheism. His change of heart has no doubt given pause to many of his followers.

Unfortunately, it takes the man on the street a long time to catch up with current philosophical debate about God or the state of New Testament scholarship. The Internet is teeming with voices claiming that Christianity is simply a myth, that Jesus did it all for the money, or that He never even existed – views that not even atheist New Testament scholars will agree with today.

Finally, if some of our critics (Flew is not the only one) have accepted the facts of the resurrection and turned to God, then others can as well. The facts presented in this chapter to support the resurrection are authoritative evidence for the claims of the New Testament. Once these facts are analyzed and understood, it's a short walk from there to the cross.

CHAPTER SIX

The Bible

"After I set out to refute Christianity intellectually and couldn't, I came to the conclusion the Bible was true and Jesus Christ was God's Son.

-Josh McDowell

Most Christians learn a lot about the Bible growing up in church. We learn history from the Old Testament and Parables from the New Testament. We learn where the books are located so we can quickly flip there when the Sunday school teacher calls out a passage. We learn other interesting facts like the number of books in the Old and New Testaments, the number of chapters, the number of times Heaven is mentioned, and how popular clichés like "cleanliness is next to Godliness" are never mentioned.

I did all of these things growing up in church and I loved it! But none of them prepared me to answer even the simplest question when first challenged on the reliability of the Bible. That is why it's important to review this subject and know a few key facts. You do not want someone to convince you, using half-truths, that the Bible is an unreliable book of myths that cannot be trusted.

Bible authenticity can be a very technical subject, so I will keep it simple by answering a few key objections that you are sure to hear in a conversation with a Bible skeptic. These questions and answers will help you better defend the Bible against false claims.

Hasn't the Bible been rewritten and re-copied so many times through the years that it can't be trusted?

This is totally false. The Bible has not been copied from copies and rewritten each generation. This is the way skeptics like to criticize the Bible on internet blogs and college classrooms. They use the example of the telephone game, where you tell one person in the room some fact and by the time it passes around the room the fact gets totally distorted. This analogy does not describe how the Bible was transmitted or translated throughout history, or the methods available to test the accuracy of the text. In the telephone game, the person at the end of the line gets the distorted message and has no way to verify if the message is accurate. Imagine if that person could get up and walk over to the second person in line and get the information from him. Surely, the second person in line should have a much more accurate account of the message than the 20th person in line. This is how it works with the text of the Bible!

Since we have ancient copies of the Old and New Testaments, we can compare those to present day copies and determine if they match. We do not have to rely on a copy of a copy of a copy and hope it is accurate. We have ancient copies to compare to current copies, so whatever happened in between is irrelevant. As a result, we know we have an accurate copy of the scriptures. Therefore, the telephone game analogy falls apart when compared with the facts.

Another fact to point out is that modern versions were not translated from older versions. For example, new versions of the Bible, like the New King James (1982), were not translated from the King James (1611). We do not translate from a translation of a translation of a translation. This is a common misconception. The New King James Version, like the NIV or ESV, was translated from the ancient Greek versions in one step. How do we know the ancient Greek versions are accurate? Because we have almost 6000 ancient copies in Greek. Furthermore, the oldest fragment dates to 117AD! There are older fragments, but they are still in the lengthy process of verification. In addition, if you include all the ancient copies in other languages, the number rises to around 24,000 copies.

With this many different copies from different geographical regions, we can be certain that any errors in the copies can be found and corrected. Moreover, the vast majority of 'errors' are very minor spelling mistakes or smudged characters. Also, keep in mind that no other ancient work comes close to the New Testament in surviving copies. In almost all cases, there are less than 20 surviving copies of any famous work from antiquity. The exceptions are the works of the Greek writers Sophocles (approx. 200 copies) and Homer (approx. 1000 copies).

Another important factor to consider is how old the surviving copies are in relation to the original text. For example, the New Testament was written between 50AD-90AD. The oldest surviving copy that is not in dispute dates to around 117AD. Compare that to all other works from antiquity, and the New Testament is again the clear winner. With all other ancient works, the time frame between the original writing and the oldest copy is from 800-1500 years. For the New Testament, it is about 30 years.

How can we trust the New Testament as a historical document?

The New Testament makes many historical claims verifiable by ancient writings outside of the Bible and by archeological discoveries. Although the historical accuracy of the Bible does not prove its supernatural claims, it would be hard to take the Bible seriously if it made bogus historical statements. For example, documents from the first and second century written by non-Christians (some hostile toward Christianity) confirm many Biblical claims about Jesus and the lives of early Christians. A short list of excerpts from some of those documents follow:

Pliny the Younger (Roman magistrate, 61AD-113AD) confirmed that Christians believed Jesus was God and described some of their practices that agree with accounts in the New Testament.

Suetonius (Roman historian, 69AD-140AD) reported that Christians were persecuted for following Jesus by the Jews and Romans as recorded in the Bible.

Tacitus (Roman historian and senator, 56AD-120AD) confirmed that Jesus lived in Judea and was ordered crucified by Pontius Pilate.

Mara Bar-Serapion (Pagan Assyrian philosopher, 70AD) confirmed the crucifixion of Jesus.

Lucian of Samosata (Greek Comedian, 115AD-200AD) confirmed the message taught by Jesus is consistent with the New Testament Gospels.

Celsus (Greek philosopher, 175AD) confirmed that Jesus was a carpenter, performed miracles, and claimed to be God.

Josephus (Jewish historian, 37AD-100AD) wrote in the first century: *"Now around this time lived Jesus, a wise man. For he was a worker of amazing deeds and was a teacher of people who gladly accept the truth."*

Like extra-biblical writings, archaeology can be used to support the accuracy of the Bible. Of all the New Testament writers, Luke reported events, people and places with the most accuracy and detail. Luke was a meticulous author who gave detailed accounts of the places he traveled and the events he witnessed. Archaeologists and Biblical scholars have documented Luke's accuracy well over a hundred times in cases where he recorded everything from major events like the resurrection to minor details such as small village names, wind direction, and water depths. In every case where archaeological evidence is available, Luke has been vindicated as an accurate and honest eye witness to Biblical events.

As with extra-biblical writings, archaeology cannot prove the supernatural claims of the Bible. What archaeology can do is add another layer of credibility to Biblical accuracy and demonstrate that the New Testament is not a book of mythology and legend, but a highly accurate account of the people, places and events recorded within its pages.

Wasn't the New Testament written hundreds of years after Christ and therefore subject to the influence of myth and legend?

Critics of the New Testament claim that it was written long after the life of Jesus and therefore it's a book of myths. This argument is based on the premise that if hundreds of years pass between the time of Jesus and the time the events were written down, then myths and legends will grow in the place of facts.

Of course, if we look at the evidence, these criticisms quickly fall apart. As previously stated, there are about 24,000 ancient hand written copies of the books that encompass the New Testament. The oldest surviving fragment of a New Testament book is dated by historians to within thirty years of the original – not nearly enough time for myths to supplant oral tradition.

Compare this to everything we know about Alexander the great, the Trojan War and Buddha, all of which was written down about 400 years after the events. However, the New Testament books were written shortly after the events described in the Bible (30–60 years), so it doesn't matter that it's been 2000 years because we have eye-witness testimony documented within 30 years of the events.

The critical time frame for ancient documents is the time between the historical events and when they are recorded in writing. If this time frame is short, more accuracy can be expected. If it's hundreds of years, myth and legend have time to grow and distort the original message.

Based on the time of writing, the accuracy of the New Testament can be trusted. Furthermore, the fact that there are 24,000 ancient copies allows historians to cross reference the documents and eliminate errors. Let's compare this to the second best preserved ancient work, the Iliad by Homer, with about 1000 ancient copies. This work is considered by historians to be accurate, and it should be; but then how much more should we consider the validity of the New Testament?

Aren't there lost books of the Bible that were excluded by the church?

No. It's clear that the books of the Bible were already agreed upon by the middle of the second century. The Bible was not canonized by a council in one meeting as critics like to claim. Critics who claim that the church neglected to include certain books or included books that were not inspired or accurate are misinformed about the process used to meticulously preserve inspired scriptures. This process was critical in the second century because of numerous forged writings already in circulation that claimed to be authentic and inspired.

The careful process of canonization used three basic criteria as a guide for accepting or rejecting Biblical manuscripts. First, the text must have apostolic authority; meaning the text must have been written by an apostle like Matthew who witnessed the events himself, or a close associate of an apostle like Luke, who was an associate of Paul. Second, the writings could not violate orthodox Christian beliefs. An example of this type of violation can be found in the Gospel of Thomas, which describes Jesus as a pantheist

God and women as unworthy to enter the kingdom of heaven unless they become men. Because of these statements, scholars universally agree that the Gospel of Thomas was not the work of St. Thomas and therefore is a forgery. The early church knew this for a fact and rejected the book as a Gnostic writing.

The third criterion for canonization was a texts' continuous usage by the church. If a Biblical text remained in use and was accepted by church leaders in diverse locations for many years, then it had already undergone a thorough vetting process that could easily expose heretical teachings. There were many gospels, apocalypses, and epistles rejected by the church in the second and third centuries (and beyond). These documents, many referred to as Gnostic Gospels, were unable to meet the stringent conditions for authenticating Biblical documents. These writings include the Gospel of Mary, the Gospel of Philip, the Gospel of Judas, and the apocalypse of Stephen.

Is there any evidence of Biblical inspiration?

The evidence presented up to this point demonstrates the authenticity of the Bible and its reliability as an ancient document. However, none of this makes a case for the Bible as the inspired word of God. Nevertheless, we can make a case for Biblical inspiration based on prophecy and pre-scientific knowledge found in the Bible.

The Old Testament offers many prophecies about the fate of the Messiah. This is important to consider because these are the very things that forgeries have the least control over. These prophecies are harder to fake and more difficult to use to deceive others. There are Messianic prophecies that anyone can claim, but getting all of them right, even those outside of human control, would be a statistical miracle.

In their book, Science Speaks, Peter W. Stoner and Robert C. Newman (1976) work out the statistical probability of Jesus fulfilling only eight of the Messianic prophecies. Using a theoretical probability model, Stoner and Newman calculated the odds of Jesus fulfilling all eight prophecies to be 1 in 10^{17}. This number represents 1 in 100,000,000,000,000,000. To illustrate the mathematical odds of this number, Stoner and Newman point out how 10^{17} silver dollars would cover the entire state of Texas at a depth of two feet deep. Now imagine one of the silver dollars is painted red and you have to choose it on the first try while blindfolded. This represents a chance of 1 out of 10^{17} – a virtually impossible probability. Therefore, fulfilled prophecy makes a good case for Biblical inspiration.

Although the Bible is not a science textbook, it has credibility when it comes to matters of science. There are numerous examples that demonstrate profound scientific knowledge within the pages of scriptures. The Bible makes accurate observations about the natural world and reveals knowledge that existed well ahead of the scientific community. Some of these examples are astounding and unexplainable by mere chance; therefore, inspiration is supported. Some of the best examples are:

The Paths in the Ocean - Matthew Maury (1806-1873) was a Bible-believing Christian that took the scriptures seriously and was fascinated by Psalm 8:8:

"The birds of the heavens and the fish of the sea, whatever passes through the paths of the seas."

His career as an American naval officer and oceanographer led him to seek the paths of the seas mentioned in the Bible. The result of his life's work was published in 1856 and titled, *Physical Geography of the Sea*. It was the first comprehensive book on oceanography to be published and included charts of the ocean currents, the 'paths of the seas', which changed the science of marine navigation.

Circumcision on the eighth day – There are several examples of medical science in the Bible that precede modern medical practice, such as hand washing for cleanliness (Deuteronomy 21:6). However, an even more amazing example of medical science is found in Genesis 17:12 where God specifically directs Abraham to circumcise newborn boys on the eighth day. Now we know why.

Vitamin K is critical to the body's ability for blood clotting, which prevents excessive bleeding from a wound. On day eight, Vitamin K spikes to over 100% of normal in the body making it a perfect time for surgery. If this same procedure were performed a couple of days earlier or later, excessive bleeding and death could occur. According to Dr. S.I. McMillen in None of These Diseases (1984), it is the perfect day for the procedure.

"We should commend the many hundreds of workers who labored at great expense over a number of years to discover that the safest day to perform circumcision is the eighth. Yet, as we congratulate medical science for this recent finding, we can almost hear the leaves of the Bible rustling. They would like to remind us that four thousand years ago, when God initiated circumcision with Abraham. Abraham did not pick the eighth day after many centuries of trial-and-error experiments. Neither he nor any of his company from the ancient city of Ur in the Chaldees ever had been circumcised. It was a day picked by the Creator of vitamin K" (p. 93).

Entropy – The second law of thermodynamics is called Entropy. This law of physics states that the total amount of energy in any system that is available to do work is ever decreasing. Because of this process, the universe and everything in it is decaying or in a state of 'running down.' Systems tend to move from order to disorder. Never do we observe in nature simple unordered systems becoming more complex and ordered. The second law is evident in the fact that you have to paint your house, or buy new batteries, or buy new shoes – everything wears out.

In Psalm 102:25–26 the Bible is clear about the second law of thermodynamics.

Of old you laid the foundation of the earth, and the heavens are the work of your hands. They will perish, but you will remain; they will all wear out like a garment (ESV).

This is a clear description of the earth and the 'heavens' (the universe) being in a state of decay and eventually wearing out. This language is very descriptive of what we know about our planet, and the entire universe. Even our sun is running down and will eventually exhaust all fuel and burn itself out. Sure, the writers of the Old Testament knew that garments, shoes, and buildings wear out by simple observation, but they could not have known that the universe would also eventually wear out.

The Earth – Many people believed the earth was flat for thousands of years before the first ships sailed around the world in the 1500s. Before that time, many believed you could travel far enough to fall off the earth. The Hindu, Buddhist and Islamic holy books teach this concept.

Three thousand years ago, long before the first ship sailed around the world, the prophet Isaiah wrote, *"It is he who sits above the circle of the earth, and its inhabitants are like grasshoppers"* (Isaiah 40:22). The fact that the Earth is like a circle was only discovered about 500 years ago; yet the Bible clearly reveals this truth.

The Hindu scriptures have a lot to say about the position of the Earth in our universe. Some holy writings claim the Earth is held up by a snake with 1000 heads. The Vedas (Hindu holy book) repeatedly claims that the Earth is supported on the back of a giant turtle. In some verses, the turtle holds an elephant on its back that holds up the Earth. Greek mythology claims that the god Atlas holds the Earth on his back. Contrast this to the Bible, which says: *"He stretches out the north over the void and hangs the earth on nothing"* (Job 26:7 ESV). This is an incredible statement of fact in a time when no one but God could have revealed it to the writer of Job.

Each star is unique – In first Corinthians 15:41 the Bible makes another surprising statement of fact: *"There is one glory of the sun, and another glory of the moon, and another glory of the stars; for star differs from star in glory"* (ESV). Centuries before the development of the first telescope, the Bible pointed out that each star is different. This is a fact of science today that was not so evident in the first century. Stars vary widely in size and intensity and the Bible seems to make this clear 1500 years before the first telescope was pointed toward the heavens.

These examples show us two things: first, the Bible makes claims about scientific issues that have proven to be true; unlike the Quran's claim that the world is flat, and the Hindu bible's claim that the world sits on the back of a giant turtle. Second, the Bible and science are not at odds when it comes to verifiable scientific claims.

Can't you make the Bible say whatever you want it to say?

This is true only if you adopt a lazy and shallow view of scripture. Those who hold a postmodern view of truth – that truth is relative – will ignore the author's intent and meaning on the basis that no true meaning exists. This is an absurd method for interpreting the meaning of any ancient document; especially the Bible, where clear intent is so important.

Bible interpretation is a serious discipline called hermeneutics. When practiced using careful analysis of the original language, understanding of intent and the correct historical context we can learn a great deal about what the authors originally intended in their message. Sure, there are areas where interpretation is difficult and a careful approach is needed, but that is far from an anything-goes approach when seeking biblical meaning.

Conclusion

It is now common to hear every form of criticism aimed at the Bible. However, with a little knowledge of the Bible's reliability as an ancient text, you can easily refute these assertions. This is true because the evidence strongly supports the accuracy of the Bible. When you hear criticisms that fly in the face of this evidence, it is because the critic's personal philosophy runs contrary to scripture. They are simply failing to apply the same standard of research to the Bible as they apply to all other ancient literature. Therefore, if we throw out the Bible as unreliable, then we must throw out every work from antiquity as unreliable. Anyone suggesting the New Testament was written too long ago to be accurate, or long after the time of

Christ and therefore not reliable, is just not working with all the facts.

CHAPTER SEVEN

Strategies

*"It is axiomatic that the most intelligent people –
college professors, doctors, lawyers, PhDs, bright folk
of all stripes – make foolish and elementary mistakes
in thinking when it comes to spiritual things."*

-Greg Koukl

There are a few critical strategies you need to understand and put into practice in order to defend Christianity. Much of this knowledge is based on understanding your opponent's tactics. The new Atheists are no longer content with simply denying God's existence, they are actively evangelizing the philosophy of atheism so that you and your children will believe as they do. Professor Peter Boghossian, author of *A Manual for Creating Atheists*, is training college student's to fan out on campuses across the country and spread the philosophy of atheism by convincing unprepared Christian students that their faith is deaf, blind, and dumb. Their central argument is that blind faith is no match for science and reason. However, this is a self-refuting argument that is easy to overcome when you know a few things about the nature of evidence, knowledge, and reason.

Talking to Non-Christians

The first thing to keep in mind is that pointless arguments and dead-end discussions will not get you anywhere. Engaging belligerent atheists for the purpose of arguing is not the point of apologetics, defending the faith, or spreading the gospel. A long-winded stalemate is typically not very productive. The only time this is appropriate is in a public debate where others are there to learn. Even then, the argument should never become a brawl that reduces to name-calling. Ultimately, we are trying to win people, not arguments.

When engaging a skeptic, try to be diplomatic and inoffensive. You should be firm in the truth but with as much kindness as possible. For example, if you are asked about homosexuality, you are compelled as a Christian to call it a sin. However, you can quickly point out that it is not the only sin one can commit, and admit that you have also sinned. This may allow you to appear empathic in the eyes of the other person and not holier-than-thou. Either way, you are doing your best to take a kind and gentle approach. If the other person is so offended that you cannot hold a conversation with them, then move on before it gets ugly.

You may have heard someone say, "Never try to argue someone into heaven." This may be good advice, but keep in mind that many people actually come to know Christ through a consideration of the evidence. In other words, you may not argue a person into heaven, but your arguments may move that person closer to accepting Jesus as God and savior.

If you are bold enough to be a witness to others for Christ - and I hope you are - and you find yourself building a relationship or friendship with a skeptic, do not try to win him over on the first try. If you do, that is great, but he was probably not much of a skeptic to begin with.

Engaging skeptics is usually a longer process that consists of multiple conversations at different times. Many times it's hard to tell that you are making progress, but you may be surprised. For example, if you have regular access to an atheist or agnostic, you will need multiple short conversations about the evidence for God, Jesus and the Bible in order to make significant progress. This is typically how it works.

Sometimes you only get one shot to talk to someone about God. In that case, you still have an opportunity to plant a seed of doubt in their mind about their own skepticism. Engage their intellectual doubts; do not exchange superficial points until someone zings the other with the sharpest comeback.

Keep in mind that no matter what we do as

Christians, the Holy Spirit must be involved and draw the individual to God. All you can do is make the best case for God and let the Holy Spirit do the work. You may never know what effect you had on that person; you may be just one small part of the work that brings her to Christ.

Whether you are helping someone understand the evidence for Christianity or refuting a skeptic, you need to learn a few strategies that will help you ask the right questions and uncover contradictions in the skeptic's arguments. The six strategies that follow will help you do that when you are facing tough questions.

Strategy #1: Discover

I call the first strategy 'discover' because that is what we need to do when starting a conversation with someone about his or her views on God, Jesus and the Bible. You may already know what the person believes if you have known them for a while, but it still helps to ask a few specific questions to make sure that you are both on the same page when defining your terms.

What does the skeptic really believe? Never assume that an atheist or agnostic or some other non-believer adheres to a predetermined set of beliefs. Not all atheists believe the same thing. The same goes for agnostics. Some believe that you cannot know God; others only claim that they do not know which god is real. Some atheists believe that all Christians worship a sky fairy that grants wishes; others are puzzled by the fact that many Christians are highly intellectual people who still believe in the supernatural. So don't try to put them all in the same box, you may find yourself arguing against a position they do not hold.

Knowing what someone believes becomes even more difficult when considering the postmodern influence in society today. This thinking leads to a relativist philosophy, which argues that real truth is unknowable. Many of these individuals believe that "what is true for you is not true for me." Therefore, don't try to approach a person like this with any confidence that you know what they actually believe until you ask - and even then it may be difficult to determine.

Another important aspect of the discovery strategy is to define your terminology. Put another way, you need to force the skeptic to define what they mean by certain assertions. You can discover this by asking direct questions, such as:

What do you mean by God?
What do you mean by sin?
What do you mean by faith?

Someone may tell you they do not believe in God, but what do they mean by god? The eastern religions believe that God is like electricity, or an impersonal force that permeates the universe. Many atheists call God a magic man in the sky or compare God to a flying spaghetti monster. Obviously, Christians do not subscribe to any of these notions of God. Therefore, this should be settled up front in the conversation. The

God of Christianity is a transcendent being who created the universe and everything in it. He is eternal, immaterial, atemporal, non-spatial, and uncaused.

You may also find that the definition of sin is highly skewed with some people. Either they do not believe there is such a thing as sin, or they don't count their own actions as sin. Of course, without God, there can be no objective right and wrong. Without God, right and wrong are man-made conventions. Just remember, most atheists live as though an objective right and wrong does exist.

Furthermore, the definition of faith is probably the most poorly understood concept by the atheist. According to the new atheists, your faith is totally blind; it is no more than mere superstition. Some believe this; some just use it as a straw-man argument. In either case, they have set their strategy on undermining faith, not facts. In their own words, atheist leaders like Professor Peter Boghossian, author of *A Manual for Creating Atheists* and Richard Dawkins, author of *The God Delusion,* want to equip other atheists with the skills to attack religion at what they consider its weakest point: its reliance on faith rather than evidence.

Clearly, this is a poor understanding of Christian faith. Christians are never asked to believe based on blind faith. Keep in mind that Peter, Paul, Luke, and Jesus offered evidence for their claims. We also have evidence from science, philosophy, and history to support many of the claims of Christian theism.

One way to understand Christian faith is to consider

an illustration. For example, I believe that my wife really loves me. However, I cannot see inside her mind and know with absolute certainty that she does. Therefore, this belief I have about her love for me could be described as faith, but it's not blind faith. I have a lot of reasons to believe she loves me, accumulated over 28 years of marriage. In other words, I have evidence for this faith I have in her. By no means is it blind faith.

Therefore, when you are having a discussion with an unbeliever, be sure to discover how they view faith and what it means to them. Point out that they also have faith in many things, whether they admit it or not. Remember, very few things can be proven with mathematical certainty – that applies to Christians and atheists. That leaves much of what people believe in the realm of faith. For Christians it's a faith based on evidence, not blind faith.

Strategy #2 – Ask

One of the most powerful strategies I have found to deal with the objections of skeptics is to ask a simple question. This may sound over simplified at first, so allow me to explain. As Christians, we can be rather defensive when someone makes an unfounded assertion about Jesus, such as: "Jesus was just a mythical character based on other mythical characters before his time." Now, your first response may be to draw your sword (figuratively speaking) and go on the defensive, or launch into a response with a barrage of well-cited evidence. However, that would be the wrong approach.

Instead, consider asking a simple question, such as: "Really, can you point me to your sources so I can go look at that evidence?" Chances are, their sources for the mythical Jesus remark is from *Zeitgeist: The Movie*, which completely fabricated the claims about Jesus being a carbon copy of other previous mythical characters. Anyone can verify this with 30 minutes of research.

By asking for the source, you place the responsibility back on the person making the assertion. You will find that many times, there is no source; it was just something they heard someone else say. It's very likely they will not know their source or why they believe it's true.

For example, two of my college students were in an argument about the existence of God. The one that believed in God got frustrated and gave up. Afterwards, I asked the student, who I assumed to be an atheist, for his top three reasons why he believes God does not exist. I told him I really want to know so I could decide based on his information.

He tried to explain it to me but kept getting off subject by talking about the Bible and Christians, neither of which are directly related to the question of God's existence. Remember, if someone says they do not believe in God, then a discussion about Jesus or the Bible is off topic. First, you have to deal with the issue of God's existence, then you can talk about "who is God."

I re-directed my atheist student a couple of times asking him again, "Why do you think that God does not exist?" He finally said, "Well, I do believe in God." That shocked me. After only 2 minutes of asking simple questions, he realized he was not an atheist. I did not change his mind; I just asked him to explain his position, which forced him to fully consider his view.

The reason this is effective is because many atheists have never had to defend their position on atheism to someone who knew which questions to ask. If they are open-minded, they may think about it. If not, you will most likely get a hostile response. If so, move on.

When asking an atheist why they do not think God exists, you will find the response is based on either reason or cause. For example, the atheist may have a reason such as, "Not enough evidence exists to support God's existence." If so, you can share the evidence you have learned to argue for God's existence. If the person is angry at the church or God, then something caused them to have that attitude. You can try to explore that avenue and see where it leads.

Whether reason or cause, the strategy should be to ask non-threatening, simple, and direct questions so that a conversation can grow. Getting defensive and launching into an argument will only cause the other person to do the same, and then you are wasting your time - and God's time.

So remember, when you hear assertions, such as:

"Christianity is intolerant."
"The Bible has been rewritten many times."

"All religions are the same."
"Evolution explains where we came from."

Ask short, simple questions, such as:

"What do mean by that?"
"How did you come to that conclusion?"
"What evidence led you to believe that?"
"Have you ever considered…?"

Asking makes the skeptic think through their assertions and takes the pressure off you to explain everything. It re-directs the discussion back to the original claim and not to you. Remember, if the other person claimed something, they should explain it – not you! This can lead to a more thoughtful discussion, if the other person is willing. It also gives skeptics the opportunity to convince themselves that something is wrong with their assertion. They will see an error in their argument a lot faster if it was their discovery and not you pointing it out to them.

Strategy #3 – Burden of Proof

Remember, Skeptics should defend their own assertions, not you. Consider this example. A co-worker or family member tells you that most wars are caused by religion. Following strategy #2, you ask, "What led you to believe that?" Many times, the answer comes in the form of shifting the burden of proof back on you. Such as, "Are you kidding, do you really think that religion is not the cause of most wars!" This is an attempt to shift the burden of proof back to you. But remember, you did not claim anything, you just asked a question about their claim that most wars are caused by religion. You can calmly respond, "I did not say what I thought about it, I'm just asking for your source on this subject so I can check it out." It is very likely the person making the claim will not have a valid source. This may make them rethink their position, or at least rethink saying it again in public when they cannot offer any evidence.

Again, this claim is another myth that comes from the new atheist leaders like Sam Harris and Richard Dawkins. With a little research, you will find that a very small percentage (about 7%) of wars were fought over religion – and more than half of those involved Islam. I thoroughly explain this in my book, *Evidence for Skeptics: Answering the Biggest Challenges to Christianity* (2013).

Remember, the burden of proof should stay with the person making claims about God, Jesus or the Bible. Many times, the skeptic wants to make bald faced claims and put you on the defensive. But why should you have any responsibility to defend yourself or your position, when you never claimed anything. Just ask questions and try to get the skeptic to fully explain their assertion. If they cannot, then the claim has very little power - and they may eventually realize it.

Shifting the burden is usually a tactic to sidetrack the conversation and take you off topic. Remember to always keep the conversation moving in the right direction and on topic. Do not be deflected off topic by attempts to change the subject or place the burden of proof on you. Always be respectful and kind. You will know if the skeptic is no longer willing to continue the discussion, and that is the time to back off. However, if he seems willing to listen, then give the Christian view of the topic.

Strategy #4 – Leading the Witness

Leading the witness may be frowned upon in a courtroom, but there are no rules against it in apologetics. A leading question is one that suggests, or leads to, a particular answer. This is not the same thing as a loaded or unfair question.

Leading the witness in this context means you are trying to redirect the question to some moral issue that the skeptic already accepts as true. The purpose is to get the skeptic to admit something they already know is true that closely relates to the topic. Some examples:

Skeptic: *"My God would not send anyone to hell."*
Christian: *"Do you believe people should pay for their crimes?"*

This exchange points out what most skeptics already know, that punishment for wrongdoing is perfectly acceptable in society. Therefore, why should our concept of God be any different? The skeptic may protest that hell is harsh punishment for the minor wrong she has committed, compared to all the good she has done. But don't our own laws also demand perfection? If you stop at ten red lights in a row and then run one, will the police officer still give you a ticket? What about all the lights you obeyed? Doesn't that outweigh the one you did not obey? Try telling that to a judge.

Everyone knows that our laws demand perfection and, for the most part, accept that concept. Therefore, they should not be surprised when God demands that His laws are obeyed. No matter how much good one can achieve in life, failure to turn from sin and accept Christ as savior is a failure to follow God's Law. Is this harsh? Maybe, but it is perfectly just.

Another example to consider:

Skeptic: *"People should decide for themselves what is right or wrong."*
Christian: *"Really, were the Nazis right about what they decided?"*

This common objection to Christianity can be answered by leading the skeptic back to a moral issue that we all agree was wrong. If we decide for ourselves what is right and wrong without reference to God, then how can we condemn others for following that same philosophy? Yet everyone in civilized society condemns the actions of Hitler.

There are many other ways to use this strategy in conversation with a skeptic. With atheists, any reference to objective moral values and duties will lead them back to something they agree with in principal, which is that absolute right and wrong really exist. Of course, absolute right and wrong cannot exist without God to ground these moral concepts. Otherwise, it's just someone's opinion. This is always a great place to lead the skeptic when you have the opportunity.

Strategy #5 – Reveal Contradictions

Some arguments and assertions from the skeptic will fail because if they are true, then they must also be false. In other words, these statements do not even pass their own standard for truth. These contradictions are more common than you may think, especially when you consider they are coming from the very people who claim to hold the keys to rational thought. Of course, rational dialogue is not found in blatant contradictions. Nevertheless, it should not be your goal to find contradictions in the skeptic's assertions and then slam them to the mat with a verbal "Ah Ha!" Your goal should be to gently point out the contradictions by asking questions. Some examples:

Skeptic: *"Only empirical science can give us reliable truth."*
Christian: *"How was that statement tested with empirical science to prove it's true?"*

Skeptic: *"All religions are true."*
Christian: *"Islam says all other religions are false. So is Islam true?"*

Other popular self-defeating assertions were mentioned in a previous chapter, such as, "No one knows the truth" and "That may be true for you, but not for me." Of course, the contradictions are obvious because the skeptics are generally talking about some issue where the truth must exist. For example, claiming that all religions are the same is a huge contradiction since almost all the world's religions disagree on the basic issues. Yet this statement is made with the same appeal one may have for flavors of ice cream or a favorite movie. Either God exists or He does not. Christianity makes very specific claims, which are either true or not true. The point is, these are not subjective claims.

Other views fail as contradictions because they can be stated, but not actually put into practice.

Skeptic: *"You should not judge people."*
Christian: *"Why?"*
Skeptic: *"Because it's wrong for you to do that."*
Christian: *"Isn't that a judgment you are making about me?"*

This same argument comes in other forms as well:

Skeptic: *"You should not force your morality on others."*
Christian: *"Why?"*
Skeptic: *"Because it's wrong for you to do that."*
Christian: *"Isn't that your moral viewpoint you are forcing on me?"*

In most of these cases, the skeptic will condemn, make a judgment, or assert their moral viewpoint about your opinion while arguing that you should never condemn, make a judgment, or assert your moral viewpoint. This is a glaring contradiction that should be pointed out for the purpose of finding a better way to dialogue with the skeptic. It's possible that he may see this error in logic and agree to discuss the subject with more tolerance for your viewpoint.

Strategy #6 – Be a Skeptic

This strategy is simple: when someone starts quoting an expert - be skeptical! Remember, the people who made the Zeitgeist movie postured themselves as 'experts' in the subject. But as you already know, skepticism of their facts is the only way to discover the truth. The movie claimed that Jesus had the same characteristics as the mythical gods who preceded Him; therefore, Jesus is also a mythical god. The facts are quite different. For example, the ancient literature does not support that Horus (ancient Egyptian god) was born of a virgin, walked on water or was crucified. It tells a very different story. Mithra (Zoroastrian angelic divinity) was not born at the same time of year as Jesus, did not have twelve disciples, and was not born of a virgin, but from a rock. There is also nothing in the ancient record of Mithra being resurrected, or even dying. Krishna, the Hindu god, is not associated in the literature with a star in the east or a resurrection. There is a reference to performing miracles, but that is the only similarity. Dionysus (Roman god of fertility and wine) is recorded in Greek mythology as dying and resurrecting every spring, never around December as the Movie claims (which was not the time of year Jesus was born according to the New Testament), and never for the remission of sins. Dionysus was said to have turned water into wine, but he was the god of wine so that makes sense for a mythical story.

Remember, it's easy to be skeptical, but we are not skeptical just for the sake of being skeptical. We are skeptics because we believe in evidence. When extraordinary claims are made, there should be extraordinary evidence. Absolute proof is not necessary for every claim, but good evidence is. The case for chemical evolution is no different.

Skeptic: *"Modern science has proven life evolved from non-life."*
Christian: *"How did they do that? Where is the data? If it's proven, then why do so many scientists reject it?"*

Again, sweeping statements that generalize the facts of science should always be questioned. After all, this is science; it is not an issue of faith, so only facts matter. Be skeptical, even to the point of demanding empirical evidence, which you already know does not exist. Although empirical evidence is not required to believe something is true, or at least believe that it's highly possible, the new atheists will demand this level of evidence when discussing the existence of God, but not when discussing the origin of the universe or life on Earth. Make sure to point this out.

Remember, your skepticism is important for your defense of Christianity. You do not truly learn about a subject by just accepting everything the 'expert' says, even if that expert has a PhD behind their name. The expert has a bias. Many times what you learn from the expert is what they believe about the subject (subjects outside of mathematics and empirical science). You do not, on the other hand, know why they believe it unless they fully disclose their position and make their case. For example, Dr. Gail E. Kennedy, Professor of Anthropology at UCLA, was being interviewed on the subject of evolution. When pressed to explain the exact process of chemical evolution she said:

"The problem with those who are unable to see evolution, I think, is they don't have imaginations."

This was the best argument this 'expert' could offer. I still have no idea why she believes in the molecule-to-man theory. What if a Christian said, *"The problem with those who are unable to see the resurrection of Jesus, I think, is they don't have imaginations."* I would not want that Christian teaching Sunday school at my church.

What we learn from the previous paragraph is that being skeptical of the experts is OK. When a well indoctrinated atheist starts quoting 'experts' that claim the Bible is a forgery, or that the apostles thought Jesus rose from the grave because of hallucinations, you should be very skeptical of their expert knowledge. I think when you start to peel back the layers, you will see that your skepticism was well placed.

Remember, the source of the information is not important, only the truth of the information. So if someone uses the old argument, "What if we travel to another planet one day and find aliens who tell us there is no God?" You should respond, "Why should I believe the alien?" It does not matter who claims that God does not exist, or that Jesus was a mythical character, or the Bible is unreliable; what matters is their data and its source.

As Christians, we are not skeptical for the sake of skepticism - but for the sake of truth. 'Experts' are usually biased; but that's OK because we are all biased. The important thing to remember is that we should not accept the biased opinion of anyone without solid reasons.

Putting it into Practice

These strategies are designed to help you do two things: challenge the anti-Christian rhetoric you may encounter, and help others see truths they have not yet considered. Defending the faith also gives you the ability to share the gospel with more confidence by knowing that you can answer tough questions about your faith and offer reasonable arguments for what you believe.

Of course, we should always remember that we are representatives of Jesus and therefore must treat others with as much respect as possible. We may be warriors but we are also diplomats, and as a result, should always try to build relationships and mutual trust.

We do not learn how to defend the faith so we can beat up people with clever arguments, or spend most of our time arguing. Remember that listening to others is just as important, if not more so, than talking to them. We need to learn why they believe what they believe so we can lead them to the truth. The only exception is when you find yourself debating a non-believer in front of an audience of people who are undecided about Jesus. In this case, you need to defeat their arguments for the sake of those listening. Even so, you should exercise as much kindness as possible.

Another key to remember is that practice makes perfect. However, I would warn you that it rarely goes perfectly. Skeptics can offer up endless arguments for not accepting the existence of God or the truth claims of Christianity. Many times it's not a rational debate of the issues. The skeptic usually has a deeply personal cause for their rejection of God, and many times this rejection comes across as anger. So expect passionate arguments against your beliefs and don't get discouraged. You will not likely win a skeptic over on the first try, but you may plant an idea in their head that stays with them for some time.

The only thing left to do is engage skeptics and give it a try. Study the concepts in this book and others like it, learn as much as you can, then go out and use what you have learned. With these strategies, you may find that your approach to witnessing will become easier, less stressful and more productive

CONCLUSION

"I believe in Christianity as I believe that the sun has risen: not only because I see it, but because by it I see everything else."

— *C.S. Lewis*

I hope this book has helped jump start your apologetics education, or added to what you already know. As Christians, we spend a lot of time learning about the Bible in Church, but not how to defend its truths. I grew up surrounded by people who believed in God and Christianity, so I had no practice defending these truths. Back then, even people who never set foot in church still claimed to believe in Christ. Today, that has changed radically. Today there is open hostility toward the church led by atheists who argue that belief in God is the main problem in this world. Although this is a relatively small group, they have a big platform, and as a result, can influence many people with their message.

The good news is that we have the ability to counter this message with facts. Most people that claim God does not exist or Christianity is a fairy-tale have never had their beliefs seriously challenged. You need to do that. Just remember that the goal of this challenge is to help others see the truth though reasoned arguments and solid evidence.

Even with solid evidence, the debate between Christians and skeptics is not likely to end. It has endured since the very beginning. The first Christian apologists were writing retorts to skeptics as early as the second century. Justin Martyr, Irenaeus, and Tertullian were early defenders of the faith that sought to offer evidence for the deity of Jesus and, as a logical result, demonstrate that Christianity is different from any other religious system or worldview that has ever existed before - or to this day.

Of course, one may legitimately ask that if Jesus is the one and only God, creator of the universe and everything within, why does He not just show Himself and end the debate. That would be empirical evidence and everyone would have an answer to the biggest questions of all time. But God has chosen not to work that way; and as God, He has that right. As a result, we need faith.

"And without faith it is impossible to please him, for

*whoever would draw near to God must believe that he
exists and that he rewards those who seek him."*

-Hebrews 11:6

People have struggled against this concept from ancient times, arguing that God unjustly demands faith. Yet, people cannot deny their own reliance on faith. Even the atheist must have faith that his concept of God is true since all (educated) atheists must admit there is a possibility that God exists. Furthermore, all people, at some point in their lives, ask of others to have faith in them, or to believe in or trust them. Why should anyone make this demand on others while arguing that God should make no such demand? It is an unreasonable argument.

Apologetics is the use of historical, Biblical, scientific, and philosophical evidence to support our faith in God. But all that apologetics can do is support our faith, not replace it with facts and data. If your path to God is a one hundred mile journey, you might travel 99 miles on evidence, but the last mile must be traveled on faith. There is no evidence-only path to God. The evidence for those who know Jesus and have a relationship with Him comes from a self-authenticating knowledge. This is an introspective truth that can only be known through the presence of the Holy Spirit.

Nevertheless, the big concept for the reader to take away from this book is that Christians can live faithful lives that are obedient to God and perfectly in step with reason. We never need to leave our brains at the church door or walk in blind faith. Reasonable people can accept the truths of Christianity without ever following cleverly devised myths (2 Peter 1:16). My hope is that you will use your good knowledge and reason to help others come to know Christ and free themselves from the myths of this world.

REFERENCES

Abel, D. (2010). The GS (genetic selection) Principle. *Frontiers in Bioscience*. (14), 2959-2969.

Copan, P. & Tacelli, R. (2000). *Jesus' Resurrection: Fact or Figment? A Debate Between William Lane Craig and Gerd Ludemann.* Downers Grove, IL: InterVarsity Press.

Craig, W.L. (1994). *Reasonable Faith.* Wheaton Ill: Crossway Books.

Darwin, C. (1871). *The Descent of Man, and Selection in Relation to Sex* (1st ed.). London: John Murray.

Darwin, C. (1859). On the Origin of Species by Means of Natural Selection, or the Preservation of Favoured Races in the Struggle for Life. *Nature*, 5(121).

Dave, D. (2009). *Calculating The Odds That Life Could Begin By Chance.* Retrieved from: http://www.science20.com/

Dawkins, R. (1996).*The Blind Watchmaker: Why the Evidence of Evolution Reveals a Universe without Design.* London: W. W. Norton & Company.

Dembski, W. (2006). *Darwin's Nemesis: Philip Johnson and the intelligent design movement.* Downers Grove, Il:Intervarsity Press.

Dembski, W. (1998). *The Design Inference.* Cambridge: Cambridge University Press.

Dunn, James D.G. *The Evidence for Jesus*. Louisville: Westminster Press, 1985.

Edwards, W., Gabel, W. & Hosmer, F. (1986). On the physical death of Jesus Christ. *Journal of the American Medical Association. 255*(1), 1455-1463.

Fowler, H. (1905). *The Works of Lucian of Samosata*. Oxford University Press.

Gardner, L. (1994) *Christianity Stands True: A Common Sense Look at the Evidence*. College Press

Gates, B. (2008). *The Road Ahead*. New York: Penguin.

Gould, S.J. (2007). *Punctuated Equilibrium*. Boston: Belknap Press.

Grimes, W. (2010). Antony Flew, Philosopher and Ex-Atheist, Dies at 87. *The New York Times*, pp. 2a.

Habermas, G. (1996). *The Historical Jesus*. Joplin: College press.

Habermas, G., Flew, A. (1987). *Did Jesus Rise from the Dead?* San Francisco, CA: Harper & Row Publishers.

Habermas, G. & Licona, M. (2004). *The Case for the Resurrection of Jesus*. Grand Rapids: Kregel Publications.

Hoyle, F. (1984). *Evolution from Space: A Theory of Cosmic Creationism*. New York: Touchstone.

Kyriacou, A. (2011). Rational Irrationality and Group Size: The Effect of Biased Beliefs on Individual Contributions Towards Collective Goods. *American Journal of Economics & Sociology, 70*(1), 109-130.

Lewis, C.S. (1952). *Mere Christianity*. San Francisco: Harper.

Lewis, C.S. (1942). *The Screwtape Letters*. New York, NY: Harper & Row Publishers.

Lovell, B. (1975). *Man's Relation to the Universe*. W.H. Freeman & Co Ltd.

Ludemann, G. (1994). *The Resurrection of Christ: A Historical Inquiry*. Amherst, NY: Prometheus Books.

Margenau, H., Varghese, R.A. (1992). *Cosmos, Bios, and Theos*. La Salle, IL, Open Court.

McMillen, S.I. (1984). *None of These Diseases*. NJ: Revell.

Meyer, S. (2009). *Signature in the Cell: DNA and the Evidence for Intelligent Design*. New York: Harper Collins.

Paley, W. (1867). *Natural Theology: Or Evidences of the Existence and Attributes of the Deity Collected from the Appearances of Nature*. Boston: Gould and Lincoln.

Ray, J. (1717). *The Wisdom of God Manifested in the Works of the Creation*. London: Printed by R. Harbin.

Roy, P., Orr, P., Botting, J., Muir, L., Vinther, J., Lefebvre, B., Hariri, K., Briggs, D. (2010) Ordovician faunas of Burgess Shale type. *Nature*, 465(7295). 215.

Schumann, H. (2003). *The Historical Buddha: The Times, Life, and Teachings of the Founder of Buddhism*. Motilal Banarsidass Publishers.

Shaffer, F. (1968). *The God who is there*. Dowers Grove: Intervarsity Press.

Whiston, W. (2009). *The Life of Flavius Josephus*. Wilder Publications.

McLeod